BLACK DEMOCRACY

THE TRAGEDY OF STRONG MEN, WEAK INSTITUTIONS

OKEY EZEALA
OKO OBASI

ISBN: 9798869983114
Imprint: Independently published
First Edition: November 2023

C O N T E N T S

DEDICATION

ACKNOWLEDGEMENT

CHAPTER 1: Introduction

- The Concept of government

- Theory and Principles of Democracy

- Democracy and the third world experience

- What Democracy means to African development

- Peer reviews vs copy & paste approach

- Lessons and conclusion

CHAPTER 2 Democracy; A reality or fallacy of generalization

- Democracy and civilization nexus; the American example

- Why Nations like UK, Thailand, Korea etc modify democracy

- Democratic impact on third world economies

- Democracy and the third world mentality

- Lessons and conclusion

CHAPTER 3 The Born to Rule mentality

- The African approach to democracy

- The Government and the governed dichotomy

- African democracy and the Western interest

- Regional blocks and conspiracy theories

- Lessons and conclusion

CHAPTER 4 Electoral Umpires and the burden of trust

- Challenges to free and fair elections in Africa

- Executive government interference

- The public trust challenge

- How African voters perceive electoral umpires

- Lessons and conclusion

CHAPTER 5 Electoral guidelines and the tragedy of non compliance

- Public deception and the umpire complicity

- The laws and electoral guide impasse

- The tragedy of selective rules of engagement

- How African Umpires set rules and change the goal post halfway

- Lessons and conclusion

CHAPTER 6 Election results and the legitimacy question

- African elections overview

- The challenges to free and fair elections

- Election petitions and the public trust issues

- Voters choice and the result difference

- Lessons and conclusion

CHAPTER 7 Laws and the bench predicament

- Poor legislations; an aide memoire to electoral fraud

- The African bar approach to election matters

- African democracy and the tale of judicial emasculation

- Fundamental rights and the State interest limitations

- Lessons and conclusion

CHAPTER 8 Voter's awareness and fallacy of public participation

- How African voters are left uninformed

- Poor government attention to civic rights

- Public contempt and issues of civil disobedience

- Public awareness and the political violence nexus

- Lessons and conclusion

CHAPTER 9 Civil society and foreign interests; a tale of indifference

- The role of foreign observers in African democracies

- Why black democracies struggle to stand

- Many civil society organizations; what has changed?

- Lessons and conclusion

CHAPTER 10 Military incursions and the doctrine of necessity

- If Democracy fails, what next?

- Strong economies under the military regime

- Military interregnum; a necessary evil

- Fallacies of democracy and the military respite

- Military transitions history and the Ghana/Nigeria example

- Lessons and conclusion

CHAPTER 11 Regional blocks and diplomatic limitations

diplomatic protocols and intervention dilemma

- State's sovereignty and allied limitations on democracy

- Protocols on Intervention and interference diplomacy

- Global limitations of democracy

- The regional blocks conspiracy and interest

- African Union; the toothless bulldog

- ECOWAS and the tale of indifference

- Lessons and conclusion

CHAPTER 12 THE IMPERATIVE OF CIVIC ENGAGEMENT

CHAPTER 13 ADAPTIVE GOVERNANCE IN THE 21ST CENTURY

CHAPTER 14 THE EVOLUTION OF DEMOCRATIC GOVERNANCE: NAVIGATING CHALLENGES AND SHAPING TOMORROW

CHAPTER 15 DEMOCRATIC RENAISSANCE: INNOVATIONS AND ASPIRATIONS FOR TOMORROW

CHAPTER 16 DEMOCRATIC RESILIENCE: NAVIGATING CHALLENGES AND THRIVING AMIDST UNCERTAINTIES

CHAPTER 17 DEMOCRATIC ACCOUNTABILITY

CHAPTER 18 DEMOCRATIC PLURALISM: EMBRACING

 DIVERSITY FOR COLLECTIVE PROSPERITY

CHAPTER 19 DEMOCRATIC RENEWAL: ENGAGING THE NEXT GENERATION IN GOVERNANCE

CHAPTER 20 DEMOCRATIC ADVERSITY: NAVIGATING CHALLENGES WITH RESILIENCE

CHAPTER 21 DEMOCRATIC LEGACY: SUSTAINING THE FLAME OF LIBERTY

CHAPTER 22 African future; the way forward

- Preparing the People, shaping the mental approach to governance

- Does Africa need democracy to develop?

- Strong Men, Weak Institutions - whose fault?

- Setting agenda for the regional blocks

- How EU survived and the lesson for Africa

- The need for equal stake of all States

- Vision 2050; the great African dream

- Conclusion and solution approach

GLOSSARY

REFERENCE

ABOUT THE AUTHOR

Dedication

This book is dedicated to the glory of God Almighty; the divine source of all knowledge, inspiration and wisdom.

A special dedication to Leaders who optimized governance to improve the living standards of the governed; those are indeed the heroes of life.

Acknowledgments

In the journey of crafting this work, I am profoundly grateful to those whose support and inspiration have been invaluable. Their unwavering support and belief in the message of this book had propelled me.

- To My Precious Wife Nkechi Akuabata Okechukwu, PhD - You have been a Jewel so dear, the secret of my courage and hope; managing my home with smiles against all odds.

- To my Mentors and role Models
H.E Dr. Alex C. Otti - OFR
Executive Governor, Abia State.
H.E. Sen. Orji Uzor Kalu - MON,
Leader of Leaders & my benefactor
Hon. Barr. Nkeiruka Onyejeocha – PhD,Hon. Minister of Labour & Employment(State)
Hon. Chief Alex Mascot Ikwechegh ,Member Representing Aba North/South Federal Constituency
Gen. Charlie Okoro rtd.
Chief Emma Eneukwu
Hon. Barr. Emeka Atuma
Hon. Donatus Nwankpa
Chief. Sam Onuigbo (Odozi-Obodo) etc.

Your love and guidance has shaped my vision and dedication to virtues of humanity and egalitarian society.

Okey Ezeala
Oko Obasi

Abuja, Nigeria
December 2023

PREFACE

In the vast tapestry of democracy, the threads of compliance with electoral legislations weave the fabric of a just and equitable society. As we embark on this journey through the pages of "The Black Democracy: The Tragedy of strong men, weak institutions," our aim is to unravel the intricate connections between electoral integrity and the preservation of democratic ideals.

As co-authors of "The Black Democracy: The Tragedy of Strong Men, Weak Institutions we embark on this literary journey with a shared passion for unraveling the intricacies of democracy in the African context. This collaborative effort is born out of a collective commitment to understanding, critiquing, and envisioning a more robust democratic landscape on our continent.

The title of this book, "The Black Democracy," serves as a poignant reflection of the nuanced interplay between governance and society, leadership and institutions. We delve into the historical, political, and socio-cultural dimensions, aiming to shed light on the complexities that define the democratic experience in Africa.

Our journey unfolds through the pages of each chapter, exploring themes such as the relationship between strong leaders and fragile institutions, the challenges inherent in electoral processes, and the role of the military in shaping political landscapes. This exploration is not intended to be prescriptive but rather an invitation for readers to join us in contemplating the myriad factors that contribute to the state of democracy on the continent.

As we navigate the terrain of African governance, we do so with the understanding that democracy is not a static concept but a dynamic force that evolves with time, shaped by the actions and aspirations of its citizens. May this exploration contribute to a deeper understanding of democracy in Africa and inspire a shared vision for a future where institutions stand strong, and the voice of the people resonates powerfully.

Winston Churchill once remarked, "The best argument against democracy is a five-minute conversation with the average voter." This cynical perspective, while provocative, underscores the importance of informed and conscientious participation in the democratic process. It is within this context that we delve into the global phenomenon of non-compliance with electoral legislations.

From the bustling Wall Street of New York to the serene landscapes of remote village in Seychelles, democracy, in its truest sense, relies on the strict adherence to laws designed to protect its core principles. Yet, history reveals instances where these laws have been disregarded, leading to profound consequences that resonate far beyond the ballot box. "Black democracy" is not a term commonly used to refer to a specific political or social concept. However, it's possible that the term could be interpreted in different ways depending on the context.

1. Inclusive Democracy: One possible interpretation could be a democracy that is inclusive and representative of Black or African-descendant populations. This might emphasize the importance of ensuring equal political participation, representation, and protection of the rights of Black individuals within a democratic system.

2. Democratic Movements in Black Communities: Another interpretation might involve the democratic movements or political developments within Black communities, either in a specific region or on a broader scale. This could include efforts to advance civil rights, fight against discrimination, or promote political empowerment within Black populations.

3. African Political Systems: In a broader sense, "Black democracy" might be used to describe democratic principles and practices within African nations or communities, recognizing the diversity of political systems and experiences across the continent.

In the early chapters, we navigate the historical currents that gave birth to the term "Black Democracy." We must state quite early that the term "Black Democracy" has nothing to do with a racial connation. We also acknowledge that the tragedy of non-compliance is not confined to a particular era or region. The echoes of past incidents reverberate in contemporary challenges, urging us to examine both the roots of non-compliance and its modern manifestations.

As Mark Twain once quipped, "History doesn't repeat itself, but it often rhymes." Through case studies and anecdotes, we draw parallels between historical events and current affairs, seeking to discern the patterns that threaten the very essence of democratic governance.

Our exploration extends to the legal frameworks that serve as the backbone of electoral processes. Eleanor Roosevelt's words, "Justice cannot be for one side alone, but must be for both," remind us of the need for fairness in the formulation and enforcement of electoral laws. We assess the strengths and vulnerabilities of these frameworks, proposing reforms that aspire to fortify the foundations of democracy.

The societal fallout from non-compliance is profound, impacting not only the political landscape but also the social fabric of communities. Alexis de Tocqueville's observation that "The health of a democratic society may be measured by the quality of functions performed by private citizens" becomes a lens through which we scrutinize the consequences of non-compliance on civic engagement and public trust.

Media, with its transformative power to shape perceptions, occupies a central role in our analysis. Walter Lippmann's assertion that "When distant and unfamiliar and complex things are communicated to great masses of people, the truth suffers a considerable and often a radical distortion" prompts us to scrutinize the responsibility of media in fostering an informed citizenry.

Throughout the book, we interweave the global perspective with local narratives, recognizing that the tragedy of "strong men, weak institutions" is a universal challenge with unique manifestations in different corners of the world. Just as Mahatma Gandhi's words resonate – "You must be the change you want to see in the world" – our exploration goes beyond diagnosis, proposing actionable strategies for individuals, communities, and nations to actively participate in the preservation of democracy.

In the spirit of global collaboration, we draw lessons from diverse cultures and nations, acknowledging that the tragedy of non-compliance is a shared concern that transcends borders. As John F. Kennedy aptly stated, "Our most basic common link is that we all inhabit this small planet. We all breathe the same air. We all cherish our children's future." With this understanding, we seek to inspire collective action for the sake of democracy's enduring vitality.

As you embark on this exploration, we encourage you to reflect on the words of Margaret Mead: "Never doubt that a small group of thoughtful, committed citizens can change the world; indeed, it's the only thing that ever has." Let the pages that follow serve as a catalyst for thoughtful reflection, dialogue, and, ultimately, positive change.

In the spirit of fostering inclusivity and diverse perspectives, we encourage readers to engage critically with the ideas presented. Our hope is that this book sparks conversations, ignites controversies, inspires further research, and serves as a catalyst for positive change. We extend our gratitude to all those who have influenced and supported this endeavor, recognizing that the richness of this work lies in the collective efforts of many.

CHAPTER 1

INCEPTION OF BLACK DEMOCRACY

"Democracy is not just the right to vote, it is the right to live in dignity."
– Naomi Klein

Unraveling the Threads of Black Democracy
Democracy is a form of government that gives power to the people, either directly or through elected representatives. Democracy is based on the principles of equality, freedom, and justice. There are different types of democracy, such as direct, representative, liberal, constitutional, and social democracy.

Definitions of democracy
Here are some definitions of democracy from various sources:

- According to the Merriam-Webster dictionary, democracy

is "a government in which the supreme power is vested in the people and exercised by them directly or indirectly through a system of representation usually involving periodically held free elections".

- According to the Oxford dictionary, democracy is "a system of government by the whole population or all the eligible members of a state, typically through elected representatives"

- According to the ThoughtCo website, democracy is "a system of government that empowers the people to exercise political control, limits the power of the head of state, provides for the separation of powers between governmental entities, and ensures the protection of natural rights and civil liberties".

Democracy, deriving from the Ancient Greek words "dēmos" meaning 'people' and "kratos" meaning 'rule,' is a system of governance wherein the authority of the state is vested in the people or the overall populace of a state. According to the United Nations, democracy creates an environment that upholds human rights, fundamental freedoms, and allows the free expression of the people's will.

In a direct democracy, individuals possess the direct mandate to deliberate and decide on legislation, while in a representative democracy, citizens elect officials through democratic processes to carry out these functions. The definition of "the people" and the distribution or delegation of authority by the people have evolved over time and at varying rates in different countries. Key aspects of democracy often encompass freedom of assembly, association, personal property, religious and speech freedoms, citizenship, the consent of the governed, voting rights, protection against unwarranted governmental infringement on the right to life and liberty, and the safeguarding of minority rights.

The concept of democracy has undergone significant evolution throughout history. Historical instances of direct democracy, where decisions were made through popular assembly, are evident. Presently, representative democracy prevails, wherein citizens elect officials to represent them, as seen in parliamentary or presidential democracies.

While most democracies usually adhere to majority rule, there are cases where plurality rule, supermajority rule (as seen in constitutions), or consensus rule (as observed in Switzerland) are applied. These alternative rules aim to ensure inclusiveness, broader legitimacy on sensitive issues, and act as a counterbalance to majoritarianism. In the prevalent form of liberal democracy, majority powers operate within the framework of a representative democracy. The constitution and a supreme court play crucial roles in constraining the majority and safeguarding minority rights, typically ensuring the enjoyment of individual rights such as freedom of speech or association.

The term "democracy" emerged in Greek city-states, particularly Classical Athens, in the 5th century BC, signifying "rule of the people" in contrast to aristocracy, which means "rule of an elite." The Western concept of democracy, distinct from its ancient counterpart, is widely believed to have originated in city-states like Classical Athens and the Roman Republic. These societies implemented various enfranchisement schemes for the free male population, and while the concept faded in the West during late antiquity, its resurgence occurred with the suffrage movements of the 19th and 20th centuries, expanding democratic citizenship from an elite class to all adult citizens in most modern democracies.

In the vast tapestry of human history, democracy unfurled as a radiant beacon of hope, promising a governance system where the resounding chorus of the people could intricately weave the fabric of their collective destiny. However, this noble idea, akin to a delicate bloom, faced not only the nurturing sun but also the ominous shadows that lurked in the corners of political evolution.

Democracy, with its roots grounded in the profound notion that power belongs to the people, embarked on a journey laden with ideals that resonated with the human spirit. Yet, this journey was fraught with challenges, akin to turbulent winds threatening to sway the very foundation on which the democratic edifice stood.

As the pages of history turned, revealing the chapters of democratic experimentation, instances emerged where the lofty principles of this system faced a perilous divergence. The very essence of democracy, rooted in the equality and participation of all, was tested by the tempests of power struggles, corruption, and the complex interplay of human ambitions.

One of the defining challenges lay in the delicate balance between the power vested in the hands of the elected and the imperative of protecting the rights and aspirations of the electorate. The divergence was stark when elected leaders, entrusted with the sacred duty of representing the will of the people, succumbed to the seduction of power, forsaking the very essence of their democratic mandate. Instances of autocratic tendencies and the erosion of democratic norms cast shadows upon the noble experiment.

Another thread of challenge wove through the intricate pattern of money and influence in politics. The promise of democracy lay not only in the equal voice of every citizen but also in shielding the democratic process from undue influence. However, as the tapestry unfolded, the encroachment of financial interests threatened to taint the purity of the democratic canvas. The symphony of the people's voice risked being drowned out by the cacophony of vested interests.

Moreover, the challenge of inclusivity echoed through the chapters of democratic history. The promise was to create a system where every citizen, regardless of background, creed, or circumstance, could contribute to the shaping of their collective destiny. Yet, as the pages turned, tales emerged of marginalized voices being stifled, and the grandeur of diversity being overshadowed by systemic inequalities.

Despite these challenges, the tapestry of democracy remained resilient. It weathered storms and resisted the attempts to unravel its intricate design. The brilliance of democracy lay not just in its conception but in its ability to learn, adapt, and evolve.

The chapters that recount the challenges of democracy also narrate tales of resilience, reform, and redemption. The response to divergence became a call to strengthen democratic institutions, fortify the checks and balances, and instill a renewed sense of civic responsibility.

In the grand tapestry of human history, the story of democracy is not one of unblemished perfection but a testament to the enduring human spirit. The challenges it faced only served as crucibles, refining the democratic experiment and reminding us that the true measure of its success lies not in the absence of challenges but in the ability to confront and overcome them.

As we continue to unravel the chapters of democratic governance, let us acknowledge the complexity of the journey, the resilience of the system, and the perpetual commitment required from each generation to ensure that the beacon of hope that is democracy continues to illuminate the path toward a collective and equitable future.

The term "Black Democracy" is not a reflection of race but has also been expanded to be a metaphor for the shadows cast upon democratic ideals when non-compliance with electoral legislations takes root. To understand this phenomenon, we embark on a journey through pivotal moments in history where the foundations of democracy were both tested and, at times, shaken.

"The tragedy of our day is the climate of fear in which we live and fear breeds repression. Too often, sinister threats to the Bill of Rights, to freedom of the mind, are concealed under the patriotic cloak of anti-communism." – Adlai Stevenson

The Genesis of "Black Democracy"

The Genesis of "Black Democracy" is a term that refers to the origin and development of democratic practices and values among African people, both on the continent and in the diaspora. It challenges the Eurocentric notion that democracy is a Western invention that was imposed or exported to Africa and other regions of the world. Instead, it argues that democracy has multiple roots and expressions, and that African people have contributed to its evolution and diversity.

One of the main sources of "Black Democracy" is the pre-colonial African political culture, which was characterized by communalism, consensus, participation, and accountability. Many African societies had complex and sophisticated systems of governance that allowed for collective decision-making, consultation, and representation. Some examples of these systems are the chieftaincy councils, the gerontocracy, the age-sets, the secret societies, and the clan assemblies.

Another source of "Black Democracy" is the resistance and liberation movements that emerged in response to colonialism, slavery, and racism. African people fought for their freedom and dignity, and demanded their right to self-determination and self-government. They also developed democratic ideals and institutions that reflected their aspirations and experiences. Some examples of these movements are the Haitian Revolution, the Pan-Africanism, the Negritude, the Civil Rights Movement, and the Anti-Apartheid Movement.

A third source of "Black Democracy" is the contemporary

democratic transitions and reforms that have taken place in many African countries since the late 1980s. These transitions and reforms have been driven by various factors, such as the end of the Cold War, the economic crisis, the civil society activism, and the external pressure. They have resulted in the adoption of multiparty systems, the holding of competitive elections, the expansion of civil and political rights, and the emergence of new actors and issues in the public sphere.

Therefore, "Black Democracy" is a rich and diverse concept that encompasses the historical and contemporary expressions of democracy among African people. It is not a monolithic or static phenomenon, but a dynamic and evolving one that responds to the changing contexts and challenges of the African world. It is also not a copy or imitation of Western democracy, but a creative and original contribution to the global democratic culture.

In the shadows of history, the seeds of "Black Democracy" took root, and in the chapters ahead, we unravel the threads that connect past struggles to the challenges we face in the present.

Athens: The Cradle of Democracy

Our journey begins in ancient Athens, often considered the cradle of democracy. Here, citizens actively participated in decision-making, laying the groundwork for the democratic principles we cherish today. However, even in this utopian vision, cracks began to appear. The exclusion of women, slaves, and foreigners raised questions about the inclusivity of democratic ideals.

Magna Carta: A Seed of Accountability

Magna Carta is a document that was issued by King John of England in 1215, under pressure from his rebellious barons. It is considered one of the most important documents in the history of democracy, as it established the principle that the king was subject to the law and not above it. It also granted some rights and liberties to the free men of the kingdom, such as the right to a fair trial, the protection from arbitrary imprisonment, and the limitation of taxation.

Magna Carta influenced the development of the English common law, the constitutional monarchy, and the parliamentary system. It also inspired later movements and documents that advocated for democracy and human rights, such as the American Declaration of Independence and the Universal Declaration of Human Rights.

Fast forward to medieval England, where the Magna Carta planted the seeds of governmental accountability. This historic document, signed in 1215, asserted limitations on the absolute power of the monarch, heralding a shift toward a more representative form of governance. Yet, even as this foundational step was taken, challenges persisted in the struggle for universal suffrage.

American Revolution: A Quest for Representation

The American Revolution was a historical event that took place between 1765 and 1783, when the Thirteen Colonies of British America declared their independence from Great Britain and formed the United States of America. The revolution was sparked by various political, economic, and social grievances that the colonists had against the British government, such as taxation without representation, the Stamp Act, the Boston Massacre, the Boston Tea Party, and the Intolerable Acts. The revolution involved a series of military conflicts, known as the American Revolutionary War, between the Continental Army led by George Washington and the British Army and its loyalist allies.

The war ended with the Treaty of Paris in 1783, which recognized the sovereignty and independence of the United States and ceded the British territories east of the Mississippi River to the new nation. The revolution also had significant ideological and cultural impacts, as it was influenced by the ideas of the Enlightenment, such as natural rights, consent of the governed, republicanism, and democracy. The revolution inspired other movements for independence and democracy around the world, such as the French Revolution, the Haitian Revolution, and the Latin American wars of independence.

The echoes of dissatisfaction with representation reached a crescendo during the American Revolution. The rallying cry of "no taxation without representation" encapsulated the essence of a people yearning for a direct link between governance and the governed. The birth of the United States saw the establishment of a democratic republic, but the journey towards true inclusivity was far from over.

Suffrage Movements: Expanding the Franchise

The suffrage movements of the late 19th and early 20th centuries were social and political campaigns that aimed to secure the right to vote for women in various countries around the world. The movements were influenced by the ideas of democracy, equality, and human rights that emerged from the Enlightenment and the American and French revolutions. The movements also reflected the changing roles and expectations of women in society, as they sought more education, employment, and participation in public affairs.

The suffrage movements varied in their strategies, tactics, and goals, depending on the political and cultural contexts of each country. Some movements adopted peaceful and legal methods, such as petitions, rallies, and lobbying, while others resorted to more radical and militant actions, such as protests, hunger strikes, and sabotage. Some movements focused on achieving universal suffrage for all adult citizens, regardless of gender, race, or class, while others advocated for limited suffrage for certain groups of women, such as those who were educated, wealthy, or married.

The suffrage movements faced many challenges and oppositions from various sources, such as conservative politicians, religious leaders, and anti-suffrage organizations. Some of the arguments against women's suffrage were based on the assumptions that women were inferior, irrational, emotional, or dependent on men, and that their proper sphere was the domestic realm of home and family. Other arguments claimed that women's suffrage would disrupt the social order, undermine the family institution, or threaten the national security.

Despite the difficulties and setbacks, the suffrage movements achieved significant victories and milestones in different countries and regions. The first country to grant women the right to vote was New Zealand in 1893, followed by Australia in 1902, Finland in 1906, and Norway in 1913. In the United States, women's suffrage was granted by the 19th Amendment in 1920, after decades of struggle by various organizations and activists, such as the National American Woman Suffrage Association (NAWSA), the National Woman's Party (NWP), Elizabeth Cady Stanton, Susan B. Anthony, Alice Paul, and Ida B. Wells.

In the United Kingdom, women's suffrage was achieved in

stages, starting with the Representation of the People Act in 1918, which gave the vote to women over 30 who met certain property qualifications, and ending with the Equal Franchise Act in 1928, which gave the vote to all women over 21 on the same terms as men. Other countries that granted women's suffrage in the early 20th century include Canada, Germany, Sweden, Ireland, and Turkey.

The suffrage movements had a lasting impact on the history and development of democracy, feminism, and human rights. They also inspired and influenced other movements for social change and justice, such as the civil rights movement, the labor movement, and the anti-colonial movement.

The suffrage movements of the late 19th and early 20th centuries marked significant milestones in the expansion of democratic rights. Women, minorities, and marginalized groups fought valiantly for the right to cast their votes. These struggles, however, also laid bare the vulnerabilities of electoral systems to manipulation and exclusion.

Lessons from the Past

As we traverse these historical landscapes, it becomes evident that the journey towards a robust and inclusive democracy is fraught with challenges. The term "Black Democracy" encapsulates the moments when the core principles of representation, accountability, and inclusivity face threats from within.

Through the lens of history, we gain insights into the fragility of democratic ideals and the importance of continuous vigilance. In the chapters that follow, we will explore how these early lessons set the stage for the tragedy of non-compliance with electoral legislations, examining the patterns that have persisted through time and continue to shape our contemporary democratic landscapes.

A Day that shook the nation

The United States of America is often regarded as the pinnacle of democracy, given its extensive history of democratic governance, robust institutions, and commitment to safeguarding civil liberties. However, the shocking events of January 6, 2021, on what became known as a Day That Shook the Nation, reverberated globally, prompting reflection on the stability of democracies, especially those with less resilient foundations.

Even from my home in Umuahia, Abia State, I couldn't escape the news that unfolded that day. The disturbing images of a mob storming Capitol Hill while Congress members sought refuge left an indelible mark. Witnessing such an unprecedented event in what is considered the world's greatest democracy raised concerns about the vulnerabilities of democracies elsewhere.

As I scrolled through social media flooded with real-time

videos, the tension and confusion were palpable. It was surreal to witness the rapid spiraling out of control, and the thought of what could have occurred if the rioters had reached members of Congress sent shivers down my spine.

The attack on Congress was fueled by the conviction of some that the 2020 presidential election was marred by fraud, leading to the unjust denial of victory to their preferred candidate. This belief, exacerbated by political leaders' rhetoric, conspiracy theories, and misinformation, culminated in a violent assault on the Capitol.

On that fateful afternoon, supporters of then-President Donald Trump gathered near the U.S. Capitol, intent on disrupting the certification of electoral votes. The clashes with Capitol police, breaching of barricades, and vandalism of the complex underscored the severity of the situation. Congress members sought refuge, and amid the chaos, a protester lost their life, while over 100 law enforcement officers sustained injuries. This shocking episode raised pertinent questions about the resilience of democracies in the face of internal challenges.

At a rally on the Ellipse, one mile from the Capitol, Trump, alleging election fraud, urged Vice President Pence to reject certain electoral votes during the certification process. Trump declared to his supporters, "We're going to walk down to the Capitol," emphasizing the need to "fight like hell" to overturn the election results.

Shortly after Trump's speech, thousands marched towards the Capitol, clashing with police. By 2 p.m., the mob breached police barricades, entering the Capitol, where they damaged property and invaded congressional offices. The Senate and House, in the midst of debating objections to electoral votes, adjourned, with Vice President Pence evacuated from the Senate chambers. Members of Congress sought refuge in various locations.

Rioters looted and ransacked offices, including House Speaker Nancy Pelosi's, invaded the Senate chamber, and posed for photos. Around 2 p.m., Acting Defense Secretary Chris Miller mobilized 1,100 members of the D.C. National Guard. By 4 p.m., President Trump, in a social media video, repeated false claims of election fraud but urged supporters to "go home in peace."

At 8 p.m., the Capitol was declared free of rioters, and Congress resumed its session at the urging of Vice President Pence and Speaker Pelosi. The Electoral College win of Joe Biden was confirmed at 3:24 a.m. the next day.

Due to the fact its objective was to obstruct a duly elected president from taking office, the incident was widely labeled as an insurrection or an attempted coup d'état. Both the Federal Bureau of Investigation (FBI) and other law enforcement agencies classified it as an act of domestic terrorism. Donald Trump faced impeachment by the Democratic-led House of Representatives for incitement of insurrection, based on a speech he delivered before the attack. In the speech, he encouraged a sizable crowd of his supporters near the White House to march to the Capitol and violently oppose Congress's certification of Biden's victory.

On January 13, 2021, President Trump was impeached for incitement of insurrection, with 10 House Republicans voting in favor. In the Senate trial, Trump was found not guilty, though seven Republican senators voted to convict. Despite impeachment by the House, Trump was later acquitted by the Senate.

In July 2021, Speaker Pelosi established a bipartisan House select committee to investigate the January 6 riot, similar to the one formed after the September 11 attacks. On December 19, 2022, the committee voted to refer Trump and others to the Justice Department for potential criminal charges, including incitement or aiding an insurrection.

By December 2022, at least 964 individuals had been arrested and charged, marking the largest criminal investigation in the history of the U.S. Justice Department.

In the aftermath, it was difficult to process. So many questions around how security failed and how the conflict was inflamed. Fingers pointed everywhere as the investigation dragged on. Two years later and we're still learning new details from the congressional hearings on what really went down.

Regardless of political views, I think we can all agree the violence crossed a serious line. Our system relies on the peaceful transfer of power, so subverting an election has consequences. But justice is a slow process, and wounds from that day will take time to truly heal. All any of us can do is have faith the facts will come to light and those responsible will be held accountable.

Mostly though, I just hope we learn from this and commit to upholding our democracy's core principles going forward - no matter who's in charge. The stability of our democracy depends on agreeing to play by the same fundamental rules, even when we don't always like the outcome. That is the true essence of Black Democracy.

 What Democracy means to African Development

Democracy plays a significant role in African development by providing a framework for political participation, inclusivity, and accountability. Here are some key ways in which democracy contributes to African development:

1. Political Stability: Democratic systems promote political stability by allowing peaceful transitions of power through free and fair elections. This stability creates an environment

conducive to economic growth and development, as it fosters investor confidence and reduces the risk of conflicts and instability.

2. Citizen Empowerment: Democracy ensures that citizens have the right to participate in decision-making processes and have a say in shaping policies that affect their lives. This empowerment enables individuals to hold their leaders accountable, demand transparency, and actively engage in the development agenda of their countries.

3. Rule of Law and Human Rights: Democracy is closely linked to the rule of law and the protection of human rights. Democratic systems emphasize the importance of upholding fundamental freedoms, such as freedom of speech, assembly, and the press. These rights provide a platform for citizens to express their opinions, contribute to public discourse, and challenge any abuses of power.

4. Economic Development: Democracy promotes economic development by fostering a conducive business environment, encouraging entrepreneurship, and attracting foreign investment. Transparency, accountability, and the rule of law create a level playing field for businesses, stimulate innovation, and enable economic growth.

5. Social Inclusion: Democracy aims to ensure that the voices and interests of all citizens, regardless of their

ethnicity, gender, religion, or socioeconomic background, are represented and considered in decision-making processes. By promoting social inclusion, democracy helps address historical inequalities, reduce social tensions, and promote more equitable development.

6. Governance and Anti-Corruption Efforts: Democratic systems provide mechanisms for checks and balances, separation of powers, and the fight against corruption. Effective governance structures and accountability mechanisms contribute to reducing corruption, improving public service delivery, and ensuring that resources are allocated efficiently and fairly.

However, it is important to note that the realization of democracy's potential for African development is influenced by various factors, including the strength of democratic institutions, the quality of governance, socio-economic conditions, historical legacies, and external influences. It is an ongoing process that requires continuous efforts to strengthen democratic institutions, promote civic education, and build a culture of democratic values and norms.

The relationship between democracy and African development is a complex and multifaceted topic. Democracy, at its core, is a political system characterized by representative governance, free and fair elections, protection of individual rights, and the rule of law. Its impact on development in Africa is influenced by various factors and dynamics specific to the continent. Here are some key considerations:

1. Participation and Inclusivity:

- Democracy fosters citizen participation in decision-making processes. In the context of African development, active citizen involvement can contribute to more inclusive policies that address the diverse needs of the population.

2. Accountability and Transparency:

- Democratic governance promotes accountability and transparency in government institutions. This can help mitigate corruption and mismanagement of resources, fostering an environment conducive to sustainable development.

3. Rule of Law and Institutions:

- Democracy emphasizes the rule of law, and strong institutions are essential for economic and social development. A democratic system that upholds the rule of law contributes to a stable and predictable environment for businesses and citizens alike.

4. Conflict Resolution:

- Democracies often provide peaceful mechanisms for conflict resolution. In regions with a history of instability, democratic institutions can play a crucial role in promoting stability and creating conditions for economic growth.

5. Human Rights and Social Justice:

- Democratic systems are designed to protect individual rights and promote social justice. This emphasis on human rights can lead to policies that address inequality, discrimination, and social injustices, contributing to sustainable development.

6. Economic Policies and Innovation:

- Democratic governments are accountable to their citizens, and their economic policies can be influenced by the needs and aspirations of the people. This responsiveness may lead to policies that foster innovation, entrepreneurship, and economic growth.

7. Global Cooperation:

- Democratic nations often engage in international cooperation. African democracies can benefit from collaboration with other democratic nations, leading to opportunities for trade, investment, and shared knowledge that supports development.

8. Challenges and Considerations:

- While democracy offers numerous advantages, it's essential to recognize that the transition to democratic governance can face challenges. These challenges may include issues related to political instability, corruption, and the need for strong institutional frameworks.

Democracy is a complex and contested concept that has different meanings and implications for different people and contexts. In general, democracy can be understood as a system of government that allows citizens to participate in decision-making processes and hold their leaders accountable. Democracy can also be seen as a value or a goal that promotes human rights, dignity, equality, and justice.

For Africa, democracy has been both a challenge and an opportunity for development. On one hand, democracy can foster development by creating a conducive environment for economic growth, social welfare, and political stability. Democracy can also empower citizens to demand better services, policies, and governance from their leaders. On the other hand, democracy can hinder development by creating conflicts, instability, and violence, especially in contexts where there are deep divisions, inequalities, and grievances. Democracy can also be manipulated, corrupted, or undermined by elites, interest groups, or external actors who seek to maintain or gain power and resources.

Peer reviews vs the copy-and-paste approach
Peer reviews and the copy-and-paste approach represent two different approaches to democracy, each with its own lessons and implications. They are two different ways of adopting or adapting democracy in different contexts. Peer reviews

involve a process of mutual learning and evaluation among peers, while copy and paste approaches involve a direct imitation or transplantation of a model of democracy from one context to another.

1. Peer Reviews: Peer reviews involve countries assessing and evaluating each other's democratic practices to promote accountability, transparency, and improvement. This approach encourages dialogue, learning, and sharing best practices among nations. Through peer reviews, countries can identify areas of weakness, receive constructive feedback, and work towards enhancing their democratic systems. The lessons from peer reviews include:

a. Learning from Success Stories: Peer reviews provide an opportunity for countries to learn from successful democratic experiences in other nations. By studying and adopting effective policies, institutions, and practices, countries can strengthen their democratic systems and promote development.

b. Addressing Weaknesses: Peer reviews help countries identify weaknesses and gaps in their democratic processes. By receiving feedback and recommendations from their peers, countries can take steps to address these shortcomings and improve their governance systems.

c. Building Partnerships: Peer reviews foster cooperation

and partnerships among countries. By engaging in constructive dialogue and sharing experiences, nations can build networks and alliances that promote democratic values and principles.

d. Accountability and Transparency: Peer reviews contribute to accountability and transparency in democratic processes. Countries are held accountable by their peers, and the constructive criticism received during the review process helps ensure transparency and fairness in governance.

2. Copy-and-Paste Approach: The copy-and-paste approach involves adopting democratic models or practices from other countries without considering the local context, culture, or specific needs of the society. This approach can have limitations and negative consequences. The lessons from the copy-and-paste approach include:

a. Cultural Relevance: Democracy should be tailored to the specific cultural, historical, and socio-economic context of each country. Blindly copying democratic models from other nations may not account for these unique factors, leading to a lack of ownership and potential challenges in implementation.

b. Institutional Capacity: The success of a democratic system relies on the strength and capacity of institutions. Simply copying democratic practices without building the necessary institutions and ensuring their functionality may result in ineffective governance and weak democratic processes.

c. Local Participation and Ownership: Democracy should encourage active citizen participation and ownership. A copy-and-paste approach may undermine local participation by imposing external models that do not resonate with the aspirations and needs of the population.

d. Sustainable Development: Sustainable development requires democratic systems that are responsive to local needs and challenges. A copy-and-paste approach may not adequately address the specific socio-economic and development priorities of a country, hindering long-term progress.

Peer reviews can be seen as a more participatory, flexible, and context-sensitive way of promoting democracy, as they allow for dialogue, feedback, and improvement among peers who share common values, challenges, and goals. Peer reviews can also foster a sense of ownership, accountability, and legitimacy among the participants, as they are involved in setting the standards, criteria, and indicators of democratic performance. However, peer reviews can also face some limitations and challenges, such as:

- The lack of enforceability and sanctioning mechanisms,

which can reduce the effectiveness and credibility of peer reviews.

- The potential bias and influence of dominant or powerful peers, which can undermine the fairness and objectivity of peer reviews.

- The difficulty of ensuring the representation and participation of diverse and marginalized groups, which can limit the inclusiveness and responsiveness of peer reviews.

Copy and paste approaches can be seen as a more efficient, standardized, and universal way of implementing democracy, as they rely on a proven or established model of democracy that can be easily replicated or transferred from one context to another. Copy and paste approaches can also benefit from the expertise, support, and recognition of external actors, such as donors, international organizations, or influential countries. However, copy and paste approaches can also have some drawbacks and risks, such as:

- The lack of fit and relevance of the model of democracy to the local context, culture, and needs, which can cause resistance, conflict, or failure.

- The loss of autonomy and sovereignty of the recipient country or community, which can erode their agency and dignity.

- The possibility of creating or reinforcing inequalities, dependencies, or hegemonies, which can hamper the development and diversity of democracy.

Therefore, the lessons and conclusion that can be drawn from comparing peer reviews and copy and paste approaches to democracy are:

- There is no single or best way of adopting or adapting democracy, as different contexts may require different strategies and methods.
- The choice of approach should be based on a careful and comprehensive analysis of the strengths, weaknesses, opportunities, and threats of each option, as well as the preferences, expectations, and aspirations of the stakeholders involved.
- The success of any approach depends on the commitment, cooperation, and communication of the actors involved, as well as the availability and accessibility of resources, information, and support.
- The evaluation and improvement of any approach should be based on a continuous and participatory process of learning, feedback, and innovation, as well as the respect and recognition of the diversity and dynamism of democracy.

In conclusion, peer reviews offer valuable opportunities for countries to learn from each other, strengthen democratic systems, and promote development. However, the copy-and-paste approach to democracy can have limitations if it fails to consider local context, cultural relevance, and the need for institutional capacity and citizen participation. It is important to strike a balance between learning from others and tailoring democratic practices to suit the specific needs and aspirations of each society.

Therefore, the link between democracy and development in Africa is not straightforward or deterministic. It depends on various factors, such as the quality and type of democracy, the level and nature of development, the historical and cultural context, and the role of domestic and international actors. There is no one-size-fits-all model of democracy or development that can be applied to Africa. Rather, each African country needs to find its own path and pace of democratic and developmental transformation, based on its own realities, aspirations, and potentials.

In conclusion, democracy can play a pivotal role in shaping the development trajectory of African nations. However, the effectiveness of democracy in promoting development depends on the context-specific implementation of democratic principles, the strength of institutions, and the commitment of leaders to the well-being of their citizens.

CHAPTER 2

DEMOCRACY; A REALITY OR FALLACY

OF GENERALIZATION

"The only thing new in the world is the history you don't know." – Harry S. Truman

Introduction:

Democracy is often considered a universal ideal, promoting political freedom, citizen participation, and inclusive governance. However, the implementation and impact of democracy can vary across different nations and regions. This chapter explores the complexities of democracy as a reality or fallacy of generalization, examining its relationship with civilization, examples from the United States, modifications in nations like the UK, Thailand, and Korea, its impact on third world economies, and the influence of the third world mentality. The chapter concludes with lessons learned.

Democracy is a widely embraced political system that embodies values such as political freedom, citizen participation, and inclusive governance. However, the implementation and impact of democracy can vary across nations, challenging the notion of a standardized democratic model. This essay explores the reality or fallacy of generalizing democracy by examining its relationship with civilization, examples of modifications in nations like the UK, Thailand, and Korea, the impact of democracy on third world economies, and the influence of the third world mentality. Ultimately, lessons are drawn to provide a nuanced understanding of democracy and its complexities.

Democracy and Civilization Nexus: The American Example:

The United States serves as an influential example of a democratic nation with a longstanding democratic tradition. It is often argued that democracy is an essential element of civilization, intertwined with societal progress. The American experience demonstrates how democratic governance has evolved alongside the advancement of civil society and individual liberties. However, it is important to recognize that the American example also reveals challenges and limitations within democratic systems. This highlights the need to critically examine the relationship between democracy and civilization, considering both the positive and negative aspects.

Why Nations Modify Democracy:

Various nations, such as the United Kingdom, Thailand, and Korea, have modified democratic systems to suit their unique contexts. These modifications can be attributed to several factors. First, nations may seek to strike a balance between democratic principles and other societal values, such as tradition or stability. For instance, the UK's constitutional monarchy is a modification that accommodates both democratic governance and the preservation of the monarchy. Second, specific challenges faced by nations, such as regional tensions or historical divisions, may necessitate adaptations to democratic systems to ensure social cohesion and political stability. Finally, modifications can also arise from a desire to address the limitations or inefficiencies of democratic institutions. These examples highlight the adaptability and flexibility of democracy, challenging the idea of a one-size-fits-all approach.

Democratic Impact on Third World Economies:

The impact of democracy on third world economies is a complex and debated topic. While democracy is often assumed to foster economic development, the relationship is not straightforward. Various factors influence the democratic impact on third world economies, including institutional capacity, governance quality, and external influences. While some studies suggest a positive correlation between democracy and economic growth, others highlight challenges such as political instability, corruption, and policy gridlock that can hinder economic progress. It is crucial to understand the nuanced dynamics and avoid overgeneralization when assessing the democratic impact on third world economies.

Democracy and the Third World Mentality:

The concept of the "third world mentality" refers to historical legacies, cultural factors, and socio-economic conditions that shape attitudes and behaviors towards democratic processes in third world nations. These mentalities can pose challenges to effective governance and citizen participation. Factors such as a history of colonization, weak institutions, and socio-economic disparities can influence the perception and practice of democracy. Overcoming these mentalities requires targeted efforts to build trust, strengthen institutions, promote civic education, and address socio-economic inequalities. It is crucial to recognize the complexities and nuances of the third world mentality when assessing the prospects of democracy in these contexts.

Lessons and Conclusion:

The discussion of democracy as a reality or fallacy of generalization yields several important lessons. First, democracy should be understood as a contextual concept, adaptable to suit the unique historical, cultural, and socio-political circumstances of each nation. Second, the impact of democracy on economic development is multifaceted, influenced by various factors beyond the political system itself. Third, addressing the challenges associated with the third world mentality requires a comprehensive approach that encompasses institutional strengthening, civic engagement, and socio-economic development. Overall, a nuanced understanding of democracy is necessary, recognizing its complexities and the need for continuous reflection, learning, and improvement in the pursuit of democratic ideals.

As we delve deeper into the annals of history, the echoes of past challenges reverberate through the corridors of time, connecting the struggles of different eras in an intricate dance. Chapter 2, "Echoes across Eras," aims to unravel the threads that bind historical instances of non-compliance with electoral legislations, shedding light on patterns that persist across centuries.

The connection between electoral reform and public trust in electoral institutions necessitates an examination of whether reform contributes to increased confidence in electoral processes and outcomes and, if so, under what circumstances.

Revisiting Past Non-Compliance

1. The Populares and Optimates in Ancient Rome

The Populares and Optimates were two principal patrician political groups during the later Roman Republic from about 133 to 27 BC. The members of both groups belonged to the wealthier classes. The Optimates were the dominant group in the Senate, and they were concerned with the "best men". The Populares, on the other hand, were on the side of "the people". They sought popular support against the dominant oligarchy, either in the interests of the people themselves or in furtherance of their own personal ambitions. The two groups differed chiefly in their methods: the Optimates tried to uphold the oligarchy, while the Populares sought to increase their power by seeking tribunician support for their measures in the tribal assembly. The Populares were labelled "demagogues" by their opponents.

In the Roman Republic, the political divide between the Populares and Optimates led to a struggle for power that often bypassed established norms. The Populares and Optimates were two political groups in the late Roman Republic that had different views on the role of the Senate and the people. The Populares wanted to give more power to the popular assemblies and the plebeians, while the Optimates wanted to preserve the authority of the Senate and the patricians. The Populares often used the tribunes of the plebs to pass their reforms, while the Optimates relied on the consuls and the senators to block them. The conflict between the two groups was not based on clear-cut ideologies or parties, but rather on personal ambitions and interests. Some of the most famous leaders of the Populares were the Gracchi brothers, Marius, Caesar, and Antony, while some of the most prominent Optimates were Sulla, Cato, Pompey, and Cicero. The struggle between the Populares and Optimates contributed to the decline of the Roman Republic and the rise of the Roman Empire. Non-compliance with electoral regulations became a tool in this power struggle, laying the groundwork for future challenges to the democratic process.

2. The Medici Influence in Renaissance Florence

The Medici family had a major influence on the growth of the Italian Renaissance. They were patrons of the arts and humanities. Through their patronage and political strategy, they made Florence into the cradle of the Renaissance. They funded the Renaissance by hosting artists, commissioning art, and supporting humanism. Their patronage of major artists like Michelangelo helped create the High Renaissance.

Some of the ways that the Medici influenced Renaissance Florence are:

- They established the Medici Bank, which became the largest and most respected financial institution in Europe. The bank enabled the Medici to accumulate vast wealth and power, and to finance various projects and ventures in Florence and beyond.

- They supported the development of humanism, a cultural movement that emphasized the study of classical texts, languages, and values. The Medici sponsored the Platonic Academy, a group of scholars who revived the philosophy of Plato and translated his works into Latin. They also patronized many humanist writers and thinkers, such as Marsilio Ficino, Pico della Mirandola, and Lorenzo Valla.

- They commissioned and collected many artworks that reflected the ideals and innovations of the Renaissance. They hired architects, sculptors, painters, and engineers to beautify Florence and to create masterpieces for their palaces, churches, and tombs. Some of the artists that worked for the Medici were Brunelleschi, Donatello, Botticelli, Leonardo da Vinci, and Michelangelo.

- They promoted civic pride and peace in Florence and Italy. They were involved in the governance of the Florentine Republic, and often acted as mediators and diplomats between rival states and factions. They also supported the arts and culture as a way of enhancing the prestige and reputation of Florence. They organized festivals, tournaments, and public ceremonies that celebrated the achievements and values of the Florentine people.

The Medici legacy in Florence is a testament to the transformative power of patronage, art, and intellectual curiosity. Their unwavering support for the arts, humanities, and sciences made Florence a center of learning and creativity during the Renaissance. Their influence can still be seen today in the many monuments, museums, and artworks that bear their name and mark.

The Medici family lost power in Florence for several reasons. Some of the main factors were:

- The decline of their banking business. The Medici Bank, which was once the largest and most respected financial institution in Europe, suffered from mismanagement, corruption, and competition from other banks. The bank went bankrupt in 1494, and the Medici family lost much of their wealth and influence.

- The rise of their enemies. The Medici family faced

opposition from rival families, such as the Pazzi and the Albizzi, who resented their dominance and wealth. They also clashed with the popes, the Holy Roman Emperors, and the French and Spanish kings, who wanted to control Italy. The Medici family was involved in several wars and conspiracies, such as the Pazzi conspiracy of 1478, which attempted to assassinate Lorenzo de Medici and his brother Giuliano.

- The end of their dynasty. The Medici family failed to produce a male heir who could continue their legacy. After the death of Cosimo I de Medici, the first Grand Duke of Tuscany, in 1574, the Medici rulers became weak and ineffective. The last Medici Grand Duke, Gian Gastone, died in 1737 without a male successor, and the family dynasty died with him. The Medici lands and properties were inherited by the House of Lorraine, a branch of the Habsburg dynasty.

During the Renaissance, the Medici family's dominance in Florence showcased how powerful individuals could circumvent electoral processes, undermining the democratic ideals championed by the city-state. The intertwining of wealth, influence, and electoral manipulation became a cautionary tale for generations to come.

Patterns in Non-Compliance

1. Manipulation of Electoral Systems

- The Policy Recommendations: Strengthening Democracy is a policy recommendation from Freedom House, an organization that monitors and advocates for democracy and human rights around the world. The recommendation argues that a growing disregard for the conditions that form the foundations of democracy, such as respect for the rights of minorities and migrants, space for critical dissent, and commitment to the rule of law, threatens to destabilize the democratic order. The recommendation also suggests ways that democracies can strengthen and protect their core values, guard against manipulation by authoritarian actors, and support democracy abroad. This result shows that disregard for democratic laws by manipulation of electoral system can have negative consequences for the stability and security of democratic states and the global community.

- The Democrats' increasing disregard for democracy is an opinion piece from The Hill, a news website that covers US politics and policy. The piece criticizes progressive Democrats, including President Biden, for their increasing disregard for the democratic process. The piece claims that progressive Democrats are willing to bypass the constitutional checks and balances, such as the role of Congress and the courts, and use executive actions to implement their agenda. The piece also compares this approach to the authoritarian practices of leaders like Hugo Chavez, Daniel Ortega, and Vladimir Putin, who consolidated their power and imposed their vision once they were elected. This result shows that disregard for democratic laws can undermine the legitimacy and accountability of democratic leaders and institutions.

- The "Disregard for human rights, dignity, democratic values and justice will hurt us to the core" is a statement from Transnational Institute, an international research and advocacy institute that works on issues of social justice and democracy. The statement, issued by 251 civil society organizations, calls on the Myanmar government to respond to the emergency situation caused by the COVID-19 pandemic, based on the values of human rights, human dignity, democracy and justice. The statement also condemns the military coup that took place in Myanmar on February 1, 2021, and the violent repression of the pro-democracy protests that followed. The statement urges the international community to support the people of Myanmar in their struggle for democracy and human rights. This result shows that disregard for democratic laws can lead to violence and oppression, and that civil society and international solidarity are essential for defending democracy and human rights.

Whether in ancient Rome or Renaissance Florence, the manipulation of electoral systems emerged as a recurring theme. Those in positions of power sought to bend the rules to their advantage, jeopardizing the integrity of the democratic process and eroding public trust.

2. Erosion of Inclusivity

In both historical contexts, the exclusion of certain groups from the electoral process raised fundamental questions about the inclusivity of democracy. Women, slaves, and marginalized communities found their voices silenced, highlighting a persistent challenge in the evolution of democratic ideals.

Erosion of inclusivity is a term that refers to the weakening or loss of the representation and participation of certain groups or individuals in the democratic process. Inclusivity is a key component of democracy, as it ensures that all citizens have equal rights and opportunities to influence the decisions that affect their lives. However, inclusivity can be eroded by various factors, such as political polarization, social discrimination, economic inequality, institutional barriers, or external interference. Erosion of inclusivity can have negative consequences for the quality and legitimacy of democracy, as well as for the stability and cohesion of society.

Connecting Threads to the Present

As we draw parallels between historical instances and contemporary challenges, it becomes clear that the tragedy of non-compliance is not a new phenomenon. The methods may have evolved, but the fundamental struggle for fairness, representation, and accountability remains constant.

CHAPTER 3

BORN TO RULE MENTALITY

"The ballot is stronger than the bullet." – Abraham Lincoln

Born to rule mentality is a term that describes the attitude or belief that some people have a natural right or superiority to govern or lead others, regardless of their qualifications, abilities, or consent. People who have this mentality may act arrogantly, selfishly, or oppressively, and may resist or reject any challenge or change to their position or power.

Born to rule mentality can be seen in various contexts, such as politics, business, education, or religion. It can also be influenced by factors such as class, race, gender, or culture. Some examples of born to rule mentality are:

- The colonial or imperial rulers who exploited and dominated other countries or peoples, claiming that they were bringing civilization or enlightenment to them.

- The aristocratic or elite classes who inherited or controlled wealth, land, or titles, and who looked down on or excluded the lower or middle classes from social or political participation.

- The authoritarian or dictatorial leaders who imposed their will or ideology on their citizens or followers, and who suppressed or eliminated any opposition or dissent.

- The patriarchal or sexist men who assumed or expected authority or privilege over women, and who discriminated or abused them in various spheres of life.

- The racist or ethnocentric groups who believed or asserted that their race or ethnicity was superior or chosen, and who discriminated or persecuted other races or ethnicities.

Born to rule mentality can have negative consequences for both the rulers and the ruled, as it can create or reinforce inequalities, conflicts, or injustices. It can also prevent or hinder the development and diversity of democracy, human rights, and social welfare. Therefore, born to rule mentality should be challenged and changed by promoting values and practices such as:

- Equality and justice. All people should be treated fairly and equally, regardless of their background, status, or identity. All people should have equal rights and opportunities to participate and contribute to society.

- Diversity and inclusion. All people should be respected and valued for their differences and uniqueness. All people should have a voice and a choice in the matters that affect them.

- Accountability and transparency. All people should be responsible and answerable for their actions and decisions. All people should have access to information and knowledge that are relevant and accurate.

- Dialogue and cooperation. All people should communicate and interact with each other in a respectful and constructive way. All people should work together to solve problems and achieve common goals.

In exploring the dynamics of democracy in the African context, this chapter delves into the concept of the "Born to Rule Mentality," a phenomenon deeply embedded in the political landscape of many African nations. The discussion encompasses the African approach to democracy, the inherent dichotomy between the government and the governed, the impact of Western interests on African democracy, and the role of regional blocs amidst prevalent conspiracy theories.

The African Approach to Democracy

The African Approach to Democracy is a term that refers to the idea that democracy in Africa should be based on the specific historical, cultural, and political contexts of each country, rather than on a universal or Western model of democracy. The African Approach to Democracy emphasizes the importance of local ownership, participation, and diversity in the democratic process, and the need to balance the values of democracy with the values of development, peace, and stability.

Born to rule mentality is a term that describes the attitude or belief that some people have a natural right or superiority to govern or lead others, regardless of their qualifications, abilities, or consent. People who have this mentality may act arrogantly, selfishly, or oppressively, and may resist or reject any challenge or change to their position or power.

Born to rule mentality is reflected in some African democracies in various ways, such as:

- The manipulation or violation of constitutional term limits by some leaders, who seek to extend their stay in power indefinitely, or to hand over power to their relatives or allies. Examples of such leaders include Paul Biya of Cameroon, Yoweri Museveni of Uganda, and Alpha Condé of Guinea.

- The repression or elimination of opposition parties, civil society, and independent media, who pose a threat to the incumbent regime or expose its corruption, human rights abuses, or poor governance. Examples of such regimes include Eritrea, Zimbabwe, and Ethiopia.

- The exploitation or domination of ethnic, religious, or regional minorities, who are marginalized or discriminated against by the ruling majority or elite, or who are denied their rights to self-determination or autonomy. Examples of such conflicts include Sudan, Nigeria, and Mali.

These examples show how born to rule mentality can undermine the principles and practices of democracy, and how it can create or exacerbate inequalities, conflicts, or injustices in Africa. Therefore, born to rule mentality should be challenged and changed by promoting values and practices such as equality, justice, diversity, inclusion, accountability, transparency, dialogue, and cooperation.

The African approach to democracy is often shaped by cultural, historical, and societal factors. This section examines how traditional leadership structures and historical legacies influence contemporary democratic practices. It considers the extent to which these elements contribute to or challenge the democratization process in African nations.

The Government and the Governed Dichotomy

Democracy inherently involves a relationship between those in power and the citizens they serve. This section explores the dichotomy between the government and the governed in African democracies. It scrutinizes power dynamics, representation, and the extent to which governments truly reflect the will and interests of the people.

African Democracy and Western Interest

African Democracy and Western Interest is a topic that explores the relationship between the democratic aspirations and practices of African countries and the economic and political interests of Western countries. It raises questions such as:

How do Western countries influence or interfere with the democratic processes and outcomes of African countries?

How do African countries benefit or suffer from the democratic assistance or pressure of Western countries?

How do African countries resist or challenge the democratic norms or agendas of Western countries?

How do African countries develop or adapt their own forms of democracy that suit their contexts and needs?

Some of the main points that can be discussed on this topic are:

Western countries have a long and complex history of involvement in Africa, from colonialism to neo-colonialism, from development aid to trade, from security to human rights. Western countries often claim to promote democracy and good governance in Africa, but they also pursue their own strategic and economic interests, which may not always align with the interests or preferences of African countries or people.

Western countries have different approaches and motivations for supporting or undermining democracy in Africa, depending on their geopolitical and ideological orientations, their historical and cultural ties, and their domestic and international pressures. Some Western countries may be more consistent and principled in their democratic engagement, while others may be more pragmatic and selective in their democratic interventions.

African countries have diverse and dynamic experiences and trajectories of democracy, which are shaped by their historical, cultural, and political contexts, as well as their domestic and external actors. African countries may adopt or adapt Western models of democracy, or they may develop or revive their own indigenous forms of democracy, or they may combine or hybridize different elements of democracy.

African countries face various challenges and opportunities for advancing and sustaining democracy, such as poverty, inequality, conflict, corruption, ethnicity, religion, civil society, media, youth, women, diaspora, regional integration, and globalisation. African countries may need to balance the demands and expectations of their citizens and their partners, and to find their own paths and paces of democratic transformation.

The influence of Western interests on African democracy is a complex and often debated aspect of the democratization process. This section critically examines the impact of foreign interventions, aid, and geopolitical considerations on the shaping of democratic institutions in Africa. It raises questions about the autonomy and authenticity of African democratic systems in the face of external influences.

Regional Blocks and Conspiracy Theories

Regional blocks are groups of countries that form alliances or partnerships based on geographic proximity, economic interests, political goals, or cultural ties. Some examples of regional blocks are the European Union, the African Union, the Association of Southeast Asian Nations, and the North American Free Trade Agreement. Regional blocks can have various benefits and challenges for their members, such as facilitating trade, cooperation, and integration, or creating conflicts, inequalities, or dependencies.

The interaction between regional blocs and conspiracy theories is a complex and multifaceted aspect of geopolitics in various parts of the world, including Africa. Regional blocs, such as the African Union (AU) and the Economic Community of West African States (ECOWAS), are established to foster cooperation, economic integration, and political stability among member states. However, the influence of conspiracy theories on the perception and functioning of these regional bodies is a significant and often contentious issue.

Conspiracy theories are beliefs that some events or situations are the result of a secret plot by powerful or malicious forces, rather than the result of natural or accidental causes. Conspiracy theories often involve distrust, paranoia, or scapegoating, and may contradict or distort the available evidence or facts. Conspiracy theories can have various psychological and social effects, such as influencing attitudes, behaviors, and decisions, or creating divisions, conflicts, or violence.

Regional blocks and conspiracy theories are related in several ways, such as:

Regional blocks may be the target or the source of conspiracy theories, depending on the perspective and interest of the actors involved. For example, some people may believe that regional blocks are part of a global conspiracy to undermine national sovereignty or identity, or to impose a certain agenda or ideology. On the other hand, some people may believe that regional blocks are the victims or the opponents of a conspiracy by external or internal enemies, who seek to sabotage or weaken their unity or success.

Regional blocks may influence or be influenced by conspiracy theories, depending on the context and situation of the actors involved. For example, some regional blocks may use or promote conspiracy theories to justify or advance their policies or interests, or to manipulate or mobilize their public opinion or support. On the other hand, some regional blocks may face or challenge conspiracy theories that threaten or undermine their legitimacy or credibility, or that create or exacerbate tensions or conflicts among their members or partners.

Regional blocks may enable or prevent conspiracy theories, depending on the structure and function of the actors involved. For example, some regional blocks may provide or facilitate the conditions or mechanisms for the emergence or spread of conspiracy theories, such as information asymmetry, media bias, social media, or populism. On the other hand, some regional blocks may offer or implement the solutions or strategies to counter or reduce conspiracy theories, such as transparency, accountability, education, or dialogue.

Role of Regional Blocs:

Regional blocs in Africa are designed to promote collaboration, peace, and development. They serve as platforms for member states to address common challenges, facilitate trade, and coordinate efforts on political and security matters. These organizations are intended to contribute to the overall stability and progress of the continent.

Conspiracy Theories and Skepticism:

Despite their stated objectives, regional blocs often face skepticism and suspicion, giving rise to conspiracy theories. These theories may suggest hidden agendas, external interference, or ulterior motives behind the actions and decisions of regional bodies. Skepticism can be fueled by historical legacies, power imbalances among member states, and the perception of regional initiatives as tools of external influence.

Influence of External Actors:

Conspiracy theories surrounding regional blocs often involve the alleged manipulation or influence of external actors, particularly Western powers. Critics may argue that these external actors use regional bodies to advance their own geopolitical interests, potentially compromising the autonomy and effectiveness of the blocs.

Regional Responses to Conspiracy Theories:

Regional bodies face the challenge of addressing and dispelling conspiracy theories to maintain credibility and legitimacy. Efforts to enhance transparency, communication, and inclusivity can help build trust among member states and counteract suspicions. However, navigating these challenges requires a delicate balance, as regional bodies must also contend with the diverse interests and priorities of member states.

Impact on Decision-Making:

Conspiracy theories can impact decision-making within regional blocs. Member states may be reluctant to fully engage in regional initiatives if they perceive hidden motives or unequal benefits. This skepticism can hinder the implementation of joint policies, compromise the effectiveness of security mechanisms, and impede progress on economic integration.

Lessons and Recommendations:

Understanding the dynamics between regional blocs and conspiracy theories is crucial for fostering cooperation and stability. Lessons learned from historical experiences and the careful management of external influences can contribute to the resilience and effectiveness of regional bodies. Clear communication, inclusive decision-making processes, and a commitment to addressing member states' concerns can help mitigate skepticism and strengthen regional cooperation.

Conclusion:

In conclusion, the relationship between regional blocs and conspiracy theories in Africa is a challenging terrain that requires careful navigation. While regional bodies play a vital role in fostering collaboration and development, addressing skepticism and dispelling conspiracy theories is essential for building trust among member states and ensuring the success of regional initiatives. A nuanced understanding of these dynamics is imperative for promoting regional stability and advancing the collective interests of African nations.

Regional blocs play a significant role in African geopolitics, but they are not exempt from suspicion and conspiracy theories. This section explores the dynamics of regional cooperation and the skepticism surrounding the motives of such blocs. It analyzes the implications of conspiracy theories on regional partnerships and their potential influence on democratic processes.

Rise of Authoritarian Tactics

1. Contemporary Challenges in Eastern Europe

The fall of the Iron Curtain heralded a new era for Eastern European nations, promising democratic transitions. However, in the post-Soviet landscape, some leaders embraced authoritarian tactics to consolidate power. Non-compliance with electoral laws became a tool to manipulate outcomes, raising concerns about the fragility of nascent democracies.

2. The MENA Region: Arab Spring and Its Aftermath

The Arab Spring, with its aspirations for democratic reforms, saw a wave of protests across the Middle East and North Africa (MENA). However, in the aftermath, some nations faced setbacks as power struggles unfolded, and electoral processes were marred by irregularities. The tragic descent into authoritarianism in certain cases underscored the challenges of sustaining democratic transitions.

Technological Transformations and Electoral Integrity

1. Cyber Threats in the Digital Age

The 21st century ushered in an era of technological advancements that transformed the landscape of electoral processes. The rise of cyber threats posed new challenges to the integrity of elections, with instances of hacking, misinformation, and digital manipulation compromising the sanctity of the voting process.

2. Social Media and its Dual Role

The ubiquitous influence of social media has been a double-edged sword in the realm of democracy. While it has empowered citizens with information and connectivity, it has also become a breeding ground for disinformation and manipulation. The role of social media in shaping public opinion and influencing electoral outcomes has become a critical facet of the modern democratic narrative.

Non-compliance with electoral legislations is a global challenge that threatens the quality and legitimacy of democracy. Electoral legislations are the laws and rules that govern the conduct and administration of elections, such as voter registration, candidate nomination, campaign finance, voting procedures, vote counting, and dispute resolution. They are meant to ensure that elections are free, fair, credible, and peaceful, and that they reflect the will of the people.

However, in many countries, electoral legislations are not fully complied with or enforced, either due to deliberate violations, negligence, incompetence, or lack of resources. This can result in various forms of electoral malpractice, fraud, violence, or manipulation, which can undermine the integrity and outcome of the elections, and violate the rights of the voters, candidates, and parties.

Examples of Non-compliance with electoral legislations

Some examples of non-compliance with electoral legislations from different regions of the world are:

- In the United States, the 2020 presidential election was marred by allegations of non-compliance with the Electoral Count Act of 1887, which establishes the process for Congress to certify the electoral votes and resolve any disputes. Some members of Congress objected to the electoral votes of some states that were won by Joe Biden, based on unsubstantiated claims of fraud and irregularities. This led to a violent attack on the Capitol by supporters of Donald Trump, who refused to accept the election results.

- In Nigeria, the 2023 general elections were plagued by non-compliance with the Electoral Act, 2022 and the INEC Guidelines, which regulate the conduct of the elections. There were reports of irregularities, malpractices, violence, intimidation, and manipulation of the electoral process, which affected the credibility and outcome of the elections. Despite the fact that the Independent National Electoral

Commission (INEC) warned political parties against non-compliance with the electoral laws in the build-up to the 2023 elections the outcome of the Presidential election became a subject of litigation that ended up at the Supreme Court.

- In Europe, some EU countries have imposed restrictions on the right to vote in national elections for their citizens who reside in other EU countries, such as requiring them to register or re-register, or imposing time limits or conditions on their eligibility. This can amount to non-compliance with the EU Treaty and the Charter of Fundamental Rights, which guarantee the freedom of movement and the right to participate in the democratic life of the Union.

- In other countries, such as Zimbabwe, Venezuela, Belarus, and Myanmar, non-compliance with electoral legislations is part of a broader pattern of authoritarianism, repression, and human rights violations, which prevent free and fair elections from taking place, and deny the people their right to choose their leaders and hold them accountable.

Non-compliance with electoral legislations can have serious consequences for democracy and development, such as:

- It can disenfranchise eligible voters and deprive them of their constitutional right to choose their representatives.

- It can distort the will of the people and alter the outcome of the election in favor of a candidate or party that did not win the majority of lawful votes.

- It can erode public trust and confidence in the electoral institutions and the rule of law, leading to apathy, cynicism, or protest among the citizens.

- It can trigger electoral disputes and litigation, which can be costly, time-consuming, and divisive, and may result in violence or instability.

- It can damage the reputation and credibility of the country in the international community and affect its relations with other countries and organizations.

Global Perspectives on Electoral Integrity

1. Democratic Backsliding: A Global Concern

The phenomenon of democratic backsliding, where established democracies experience erosion in democratic norms and practices, has become a global concern. Instances of leaders bending or disregarding electoral rules within well-established democracies underscore the universality of the challenge.

Democratic erosion is a nuanced process distinct from a coup. Historically, the demise of democracies was marked by dramatic events, often involving a dictator forcibly overthrowing an elected government. However, in contemporary scenarios, it is uncommon for authoritarians to ascend to power through a coup.

Instead, democracies in decline undergo a gradual erosion. While elections still take place, legislative and procedural alterations make voting more challenging, impede serious challenges to incumbents, or hinder the translation of electoral victories into substantial policy impact. This incremental and episodic process, as articulated by political scientists Daniel Ziblatt and Steven Levitsky, involves elected autocrats maintaining a democratic facade while hollowing out its substance. Many attempts to undermine democracy are "legal," sanctioned by legislatures or accepted by the courts.

Various terms, such as "democratic erosion," "democratic backsliding," "democratic regression," and "autocratization," are used by political scientists to characterize this phenomenon.

2. Historical Context of Democratic Decline in the United States

Before delving into democratic decline in the 21st century United States, it's crucial to consider historical context. Some aspects of America's governing institutions have faced criticism for being anti-democratic or posing threats to civil liberties. Elements like the Senate, Electoral College, filibuster, and the doctrine of "judicial supremacy" have deep historical roots. The winner-takes-all representation, along with the growth of presidential power, has evolved over time.

The United States has witnessed democratic reversals before, notably during the post-Civil War "Radical Reconstruction" period, followed by the entrenchment of white supremacist regimes during the "Jim Crow" era. Achieving nearly universal suffrage required federal protection of Black Americans' voting rights in 1965. Challenges persist, with the Civil Rights Movement's successes contested by issues like expansive policing and incarceration, contributing to contemporary governance challenges.

3. Global Democratic Retreat

While the idiosyncrasies of American governance and a history of race-based exclusion create specific vulnerabilities, democratic backsliding is not unique to the United States. Globally, democracy is in decline, with more closed autocracies than liberal democracies for the first time in decades. A majority of the world's population resides in autocracies, and overall democratic levels have regressed to mid-1980s levels.

4. Democratic Decline in the United States beyond Trump

In recent years, concerns about democratic decline in the United States have been raised by experts. Various indices measuring democratic elements show substantial erosion. The V-Dem Liberal Democracy Index and Freedom House's "Freedom in the World" measure have indicated decline since 2016, placing the United States among "flawed democracies" in the Economist's Democracy Index.

This erosion predates the post-2020 election events, where the sitting president refused to concede and encouraged supporters to storm the Capitol. Despite improvements in democratic functioning since 2020, the health of U.S. democracy has not fully recovered to early 2000s levels. The democratic decline is not solely attributed to Donald Trump, with key factors being the freedom and fairness of elections and the expansion of executive power, explored further in subsequent blogs or the full report on understanding democratic decline in the United States.

The COVID-19 pandemic has worsened the democratic backsliding in sub-Saharan Africa. Many African countries are now ruled by fully or partially authoritarian regimes, more than at any time in the past two decades.

Some African leaders have used the pandemic as an excuse to extend their stay in power by delaying elections in Somalia and Ethiopia, silencing opposition voices in Uganda and Tanzania, and restricting media freedom across the continent. The security forces have often enforced the pandemic measures with violence, sparking protests in Kenya and even in more democratic countries such as South Africa.

As a result, many Africans feel disconnected from their supposed representatives. This can lead to political instability and violent conflict, as seen in Ethiopia, Mozambique, and Nigeria. These conflicts are driven by the competition among elites and the resistance of citizens against oppressive regimes, and they hinder social and economic progress for the continent's fast-growing population. These factors also contribute to internal displacement and external migration, both within Africa and to Europe. To address these challenges, it is necessary to deal with the long-standing grievances that have been neglected or aggravated by the poor and often brutal governance that prevails in many African countries.

Sub-Saharan Africa is currently experiencing a democratic decline, a trend accelerated by the COVID-19 pandemic. More individuals in the region are now living under either fully or partially authoritarian states than in most periods over the last two decades.

Even preceding the pandemic, numerous African heads of state had been increasingly undermining term limits or manipulating elections to extend their time in power. The pandemic has provided them with added leverage, offering justification for delaying elections in Somalia and Ethiopia, suppressing opposition figures in Uganda and Tanzania, and imposing restrictions on media throughout the continent. Security services enforcing pandemic restrictions have frequently employed brutal methods, sparking protests in Kenya and even in more established democracies like South Africa.

As governments across the continent, with some exceptions, tend toward greater authoritarianism, African citizens are likely to become more estranged from those purporting to represent them. This political instability may manifest in episodes of severe violence, as already witnessed in Ethiopia, Mozambique, and Nigeria. Such upheaval is poised to intensify as elites vie for power and citizens resist oppressive regimes, ultimately hindering social and economic development to the detriment of the rapidly growing population on the continent. This combination of factors also contributes to internal displacement and outward migration, both within Africa and towards Europe. Addressing these challenges necessitates confronting longstanding grievances, often exacerbated by the prevalent poor and sometimes brutal governance that characterizes much of the African continent.

2. International Efforts and Accountability

Global institutions and alliances play a crucial role in upholding electoral integrity. From election monitoring missions to diplomatic interventions, the international community strives to hold nations accountable for adherence to democratic principles. However, the effectiveness of these efforts remains a subject of ongoing scrutiny.

Navigating the Complex Present

During the "third wave" of democratization that swept across much of Africa in the post-Cold War era, there was optimism that Africans would experience the freedoms enjoyed by citizens in former colonial powers. Initial progress was notable, with a shift from two-thirds of African states being "not free" in 1989, according to Freedom House, to two-thirds being considered "free" or "partly free" by 2009.

However, both foreign and domestic expectations for liberal democracy in Africa have often proven unrealistic, and setbacks are not unexpected. For much of the continent, the foundations of a political culture necessary for sustaining liberal democracy have been weak throughout the postcolonial era, spanning roughly six decades for most African states. The persistence of religious and ethnic rivalries has been underestimated by African democrats and their international supporters. The role of the police and the army, often remnants of colonialism, has been both a cause and consequence of power systems favoring a select group of elites.

Authoritarian and semi-authoritarian leaders, cognizant of foreign opinion, have adorned their regimes with democratic forms, including regular (albeit rigged) elections and a de jure (if not de facto) separation of powers. Presidential term limits, where implemented, have often been circumvented through so-called constitutional coups. Heads of state have adeptly exploited social cleavages and stoked fears of malevolent foreign interference to divert popular pressure from their illiberal rule.

Current trends in Africa's democratic trajectory are influenced by factors such as the legacy of colonialism and the rise of the digital age. Four notable trends include:

1. Temporal: Gradual Gains for Authoritarians:

In its 2021 report, Freedom House identified only eight sub-Saharan African countries as free. Among these, half are small island states or nations like Botswana and Ghana with high levels of economic and social development. Robust government institutions act as a safeguard against self-interested leaders, contributing to stability during elections.

2. Institutional Strength: A Bulwark against Authoritarianism:

Strong institutions of government, exemplified by countries like Botswana, Mauritius, and Ghana, serve as a bulwark against self-interested leaders. They provide stability around elections and contribute to a peaceful transition of power, even in cases where electoral results are contested.

3. Legal Adherence: Ghana's 2020 Election as a Model:

Ghana's 2020 election showcased a commitment to legal adherence, with opposition candidate John Mahama accepting the Supreme Court's decision upholding incumbent President Nana Akufo-Addo's victory. This commitment helped prevent large-scale violence during the electoral process.

4. Challenges and Violence: Postelection Tensions:

While Ghana's election demonstrated legal adherence, five people lost their lives in postelection violence, highlighting ongoing challenges and tensions in the democratic process. The existence of pockets of violence underscores the need for continued efforts to strengthen democratic institutions and practices across the continent.

Lessons and Conclusion

Drawing insights from the Born to Rule Mentality, this

section distills key lessons learned from the African approach to democracy, the government and governed dichotomy, the influence of Western interests, and the role of regional blocs. It reflects on the challenges and opportunities presented by these dynamics and considers how African nations can navigate them to strengthen democratic governance. The chapter concludes by emphasizing the importance of understanding and addressing these issues for the advancement of democracy in Africa.

This chapter seeks to contribute to the ongoing discourse on African democracy, providing a nuanced exploration of the intricate factors that shape political landscapes and influence the democratization process on the continent.

As we navigate the complexities of the modern era, it becomes evident that the tragedy of strong men,weak institutions has adapted to the changing tides of time. In the chapters to come, we will delve deeper into the legal frameworks, societal dynamics, and media influences that shape the contemporary landscape of democratic governance. By understanding the challenges of the present, we lay the groundwork for strategies to fortify democracy against the shadows of strong men,weak institutions.

CHAPTER 4

ELECTORAL UMPIRES AND THE BURDEN OF TRUST

"Injustice anywhere is a threat to justice everywhere."

– Martin Luther King Jr.

Introduction:

This chapter examines the role of electoral umpires in ensuring free and fair elections, with a focus on the challenges they face in Africa. It delves into the issues surrounding executive government interference and the crucial aspect of public trust in electoral processes. By exploring these topics, the chapter aims to shed light on the complexities of conducting credible elections and the burden of trust placed on electoral umpires.

This chapter delves into the critical role of electoral umpires in ensuring the integrity of democratic processes. Examining the challenges to free and fair elections in Africa, it explores the impact of executive government interference on electoral bodies and the resulting burden on public trust.

Challenges to Free and Fair Elections in Africa

- This section discusses the numerous challenges that hinder the conduct of free and fair elections in Africa.

- It examines issues such as inadequate electoral infrastructure, voter intimidation, political violence, voter suppression, and limited access to information.

- The chapter highlights how these challenges undermine the credibility and integrity of electoral processes, posing significant obstacles to achieving truly democratic outcomes.

Ensuring free and fair elections is fundamental to the democratic process, yet African nations often grapple with multifaceted challenges in this regard. This section investigates the various obstacles that hinder the conduct of transparent and unbiased elections on the continent. These challenges may include issues related to voter registration, electoral violence, inadequate infrastructure, and the manipulation of electoral laws.

Executive Government Interference

- The section explores the issue of executive government interference in electoral processes.

- It analyzes how incumbent governments may exploit their positions of power to manipulate electoral outcomes, through tactics such as gerrymandering, biased media coverage, or restrictions on opposition candidates.

- The chapter highlights the importance of safeguarding the independence and autonomy of electoral umpires to mitigate the influence of executive interference.

One of the foremost challenges to the electoral process in Africa lies in the interference by the executive branch of government. This section explores instances where the ruling government exerts undue influence on electoral bodies, compromising their autonomy and impartiality. It scrutinizes the impact of executive interference on the composition of electoral commissions, the delineation of electoral boundaries, and the overall fairness of the electoral playing field.

Addressing Challenges and Building Trust:

- This section explores strategies and measures to address the challenges faced by electoral umpires in Africa.

- It discusses the importance of institutional strengthening, including enhancing the capacity and independence of electoral bodies.

- The chapter also highlights the significance of civic education, voter awareness campaigns, and inclusive participation to foster trust and confidence in electoral processes.

The Public Trust Challenge

Public trust is the bedrock of a functional democracy. However, when electoral processes are marred by irregularities or perceived bias, the trust of the public in the electoral system is eroded. This section delves into the challenges posed by a lack of public trust, examining how it can lead to voter apathy, disengagement, and, in extreme cases, political instability. It considers the implications of public skepticism on the legitimacy of elected leaders and the overall democratic governance structure.

Lessons Learned:

Analyzing past elections in Africa provides valuable insights into the lessons learned from both successful and flawed processes. This section reflects on instances where electoral umpires were able to navigate challenges, maintain integrity, and restore public trust. It also explores the consequences of failure, emphasizing the importance of drawing actionable lessons from both positive and negative experiences.

- The chapter concludes by summarizing the lessons learned from the examination of electoral umpires and the burden of trust.

- It underscores the need for continuous efforts to address challenges to free and fair elections, including executive government interference and the restoration of public trust.

- The chapter emphasizes the importance of robust institutions, transparency, and citizen engagement in strengthening electoral processes and upholding democratic principles.

Historical Evolution of Electoral Laws

Historical evolution of electoral laws is a fascinating topic that explores how different countries and regions have developed and changed their rules and systems for electing their representatives and leaders. Some of the main issues and sources of election law include:

- The constitutional and legal framework that defines the electoral system, such as the type of voting system, the number and size of electoral districts, the eligibility and rights of voters and candidates, the role and powers of election authorities, and the procedures for resolving electoral disputes.

- The political and social context that influences the electoral system, such as the level of democracy, the degree of pluralism and diversity, the history and culture of the country or region, the interests and preferences of the voters and the parties, and the challenges and opportunities for electoral reform.

- The comparative and international perspective that examines the similarities and differences among various electoral systems, such as the advantages and disadvantages of proportional representation versus plurality or majority systems, the effects of electoral systems on political representation and participation, and the best practices and standards for ensuring free and fair elections. We shall start our exploration with the ancient Greeks.

1. Ancient Roots: The Athenian Experiment

The ancient Athenians laid the groundwork for democratic governance, experimenting with mechanisms to ensure citizen participation. The foundational concepts of **isonomia** (equality before the law) and **isegoria** (equal participation in public debate) sowed the seeds for future legal frameworks, emphasizing the importance of fairness and inclusivity.

- Athenian democracy was not the first or the only form of democracy in ancient Greece, but it was the most developed and the most documented. Other Greek city-states, such as Argos, Syracuse, Rhodes, and Erythrai, also had democratic constitutions at some point in their history.

- Athenian democracy was a direct democracy, meaning that all male citizens could participate in the assembly (ekklēsia), the main decision-making body, and vote on laws and policies by raising their hands. The assembly met at least once a month, sometimes more, on a hill called the Pnyx, which could accommodate around 6000 citizens.

- Athenian democracy also involved a council (boulē) of 500 citizens, chosen by lot, who prepared the agenda for the assembly and supervised the administration of the state. The council was divided into 10 groups of 50, each serving for one tenth of the year. The council met every day, except on religious festivals, in a building called the bouleuterion.

- Athenian democracy also relied on a system of courts (dikasteria) to settle legal disputes and try criminal cases. The courts were composed of jurors (dikastai), who were also chosen by lot from among the male citizens. The number of jurors varied from 201 to 2501, depending on the case. The jurors heard the arguments of both sides and voted by secret ballot. There was no appeal or review of the verdict.

- Athenian democracy was based on the principles of isonomia (equality before the law) and isegoria (equal right to speak in public debate). These principles were meant to ensure that every citizen had a fair chance to participate in the political process and to express their opinions and interests. However, Athenian democracy also had its limitations and exclusions. Women, slaves, foreigners, and children were not considered citizens and had no political rights.

2. Renaissance and Enlightenment Influences

These two historical periods had a significant impact on the development of modern political thought, especially in the areas of human rights, democracy, and constitutionalism.

The Renaissance was a cultural movement that spanned from the 14th to the 17th century, mainly in Europe. It was characterized by a revival of classical learning and values, as well as artistic, literary, and scientific innovations. The Renaissance also fostered humanism, a philosophical outlook that emphasized the dignity and potential of human beings, as well as their rational and creative capacities.

The Enlightenment was an intellectual movement that emerged in the 18th century, mainly in Europe and America. It was influenced by the scientific revolution and the discoveries of new lands and cultures. The Enlightenment promoted reason, empiricism, and skepticism as the basis of knowledge and morality. It also challenged the authority of religion and monarchy, and advocated for natural rights, individual liberty, and social progress.

The Renaissance and the Enlightenment had some connections, but also major differences. The Renaissance prepared the ground for the Enlightenment by introducing humanism, individualism, and skepticism, which questioned the traditional sources of authority and knowledge. However, the Enlightenment went beyond the Renaissance by proposing radical social and political reforms, based on the ideals of reason, science, and human rights.

The Renaissance and the Enlightenment influenced many philosophers and political thinkers, such as John Locke and Montesquieu, who contributed to the development of modern political thought. John Locke (1632-1704) was an English philosopher who is considered one of the founders of liberalism and empiricism. He argued that human beings are born with natural rights, such as life, liberty, and property, and that governments are formed by a social contract to protect these rights. He also defended the separation of powers, the rule of law, and the right of resistance against tyranny.

Montesquieu (1689-1755) was a French philosopher who is regarded as one of the pioneers of sociology and political science. He analyzed the different forms of government, such as monarchy, republic, and despotism, and their relation to the climate, geography, and culture of the people. He also advocated for the separation of powers, the balance of forces, and the preservation of liberty and justice.

During the Renaissance and Enlightenment eras, philosophers and political thinkers such as John Locke and Montesquieu contributed significantly to the development of modern political thought. Their ideas on individual rights, separation of powers, and the social contract influenced the formulation of constitutional principles, including those related to electoral laws.

Core Principles of Electoral Legislation

Core principles of electoral legislation are foundational principles that guide the development, implementation, and evaluation of laws and regulations related to the electoral process. These principles aim to ensure fairness, transparency, inclusivity, and the overall integrity of elections. Core principles of electoral legislation are the fundamental rules and norms that govern the conduct of elections and the protection of electoral rights. They are derived from international standards, national constitutions, and legal frameworks, and they aim to ensure that elections are free, fair, and credible. While specific electoral legislation may vary among countries, the following core principles are commonly recognized and emphasized. Some of the core principles of electoral legislation are:

1. Universal Suffrage: Expanding the Franchise

The evolution of electoral laws has been marked by a gradual expansion of the franchise. Movements advocating for universal suffrage have played a crucial role in dismantling barriers to political participation, ensuring that citizens, regardless of gender, race, or socio-economic status, have the right to vote.

Electoral legislation should guarantee the right to vote for all eligible citizens without any discrimination based on race, gender, religion, ethnicity, socioeconomic status, or other factors. Universal suffrage ensures that every citizen has an equal and meaningful opportunity to participate in the democratic process.

2. Free and Fair Elections: Electoral laws should promote conditions that allow for free and fair elections. This includes safeguarding the right to free expression, assembly,

and association, as well as ensuring that electoral processes are conducted without manipulation, fraud, or intimidation.

3. Secret Ballot: The secret ballot is a fundamental principle to protect the privacy of voters and prevent coercion or undue influence. Electoral legislation should mandate the use of secret ballots to ensure that individuals can freely express their choices without fear of reprisal.

4. Competitive Political Environment: Legislation should encourage a competitive and pluralistic political environment, where multiple political parties and candidates can freely compete for public support. Fair access to media, public resources, and opportunities for political campaigning should be guaranteed.

5. Fair Representation: Proportional and Representative Systems. Electoral laws should strive for equal representation, ensuring that different segments of the population are adequately represented in elected bodies. Measures such as proportional representation or the creation of electoral districts aim to achieve a fair distribution of political power.

Legal frameworks strive to achieve fair representation, balancing the need for political stability with the imperative of inclusivity. Proportional representation systems, for instance, aim to translate votes into seats in a manner that reflects the diversity of the electorate, fostering a more accurate reflection of public opinion.

6. Independent Electoral Management: Establishing an independent electoral management body (EMB) is crucial to

oversee and administer the electoral process impartially. The EMB should be free from interference, and its members should be appointed based on their competence and impartiality.

7. Transparent Electoral Processes: Transparency is essential for building public trust in the electoral process. Legislation should mandate transparency in various aspects, including voter registration, candidate nomination, ballot counting, and the announcement of results. Access to information related to the electoral process should be facilitated.

8. Voter Education: Electoral legislation should include provisions for voter education programs to inform citizens about the electoral process, their rights, and the importance of their participation. Well-informed voters contribute to a more robust and credible democratic system.

9. Dispute Resolution Mechanisms: Adequate mechanisms for resolving electoral disputes should be established. Legislation should outline clear procedures for handling complaints, conducting recounts, and addressing any irregularities that may arise during the electoral process.

10. Regular Review and Reform: Electoral laws should provide for regular reviews and reforms to adapt to changing circumstances, address emerging challenges, and enhance the effectiveness and fairness of the electoral system.

These core principles collectively contribute to the establishment of a democratic electoral framework that upholds the integrity of elections and reflects the will of the people. Countries may adapt these principles to their specific contexts while maintaining the overarching goal of a free, fair, and inclusive electoral process.

Fault Lines and Challenges

Legal Loopholes: A Breeding Ground for Non-Compliance

Despite their noble intentions, electoral laws are not immune to exploitation. Legal loopholes, ambiguous language, and gaps in enforcement can create opportunities for non-compliance. Understanding these vulnerabilities is crucial in fortifying the legal foundations of democracy.

Legal loopholes are gaps or ambiguities in the law that allow people or entities to avoid or circumvent the intended purpose or effect of the law. Non-compliance is the failure or refusal to obey or follow the law or other rules or standards. Legal loopholes can create a breeding ground for non-compliance by providing opportunities or incentives for individuals or organizations to exploit the law for their own benefit or to evade their obligations or responsibilities.

Legal loopholes can arise from various sources, such as drafting errors, vague or inconsistent language, outdated or incomplete provisions, conflicting or overlapping jurisdictions, or unforeseen circumstances or scenarios. Legal loopholes can also be deliberately created or maintained by powerful or influential actors who benefit from them or who seek to undermine or weaken the law.

Legal loopholes can have negative consequences for society, such as undermining the rule of law, eroding public trust and confidence, creating unfair advantages or disadvantages, enabling corruption or fraud, harming human rights or the environment, or compromising public health or safety. Legal loopholes can also pose challenges for law enforcement, regulation, and oversight, as they can make it difficult or impossible to detect, prevent, or punish non-compliance or misconduct.

Legal loopholes can be addressed or closed by various means, such as revising or amending the law, clarifying or interpreting the law, harmonizing or coordinating the law, enforcing or applying the law, or challenging or litigating the law. However, closing legal loopholes can also face obstacles or resistance, such as political or economic interests, legal or technical complexities, or ethical or moral dilemmas. Therefore, closing legal loopholes requires careful analysis, consultation, and evaluation of the costs and benefits, as well as the potential risks and opportunities, of different options and alternatives.

2. Partisan Interference: Threats to Impartiality

Partisan interference is the attempt by political actors or groups to influence, manipulate, or undermine the impartial application of electoral laws, such as the rules and procedures for conducting elections, resolving disputes, and ensuring accountability. Impartiality is the principle that electoral laws should be applied fairly and consistently, without favoring or discriminating against any party, candidate, or voter.

The specter of partisan interference poses a significant challenge to the impartial application of electoral laws. Partisan interference refers to the undue influence or involvement of political parties in the electoral process, with the intent of gaining an unfair advantage or manipulating outcomes in their favor. This interference can manifest in various forms, undermining the integrity and impartiality of the electoral system.

1. Manipulation of Electoral Boundaries: Partisan interference often involves attempts to manipulate electoral boundaries through gerrymandering. Political parties may seek to redraw electoral districts to concentrate or dilute the voting power of certain demographics, thereby influencing election outcomes in their favor.

2. Voter Suppression Tactics: Partisan actors may employ voter suppression tactics to disenfranchise specific groups of

voters who are perceived to be less likely to support their opponents. This can include restrictive voter ID laws, purging voter rolls, or limiting early voting opportunities, disproportionately affecting certain communities.

3. Misuse of Campaign Financing: Improper use of campaign financing is another facet of partisan interference. Parties may exploit loopholes or engage in illegal activities to funnel excessive funds into their campaigns, gaining an unfair advantage over their opponents.

4. Intimidation and Coercion: Partisan interference can take the form of intimidation and coercion, where political actors attempt to influence voters through threats, harassment, or other forms of pressure. This undermines the free and fair expression of voters' choices.

5. Influence on Media and Information: Partisan actors may seek to influence media narratives and control information to shape public opinion in their favor. This can involve spreading misinformation, disinformation, or exerting undue influence on news outlets, compromising the electorate's ability to make informed decisions.

6. Manipulation of Electoral Procedures: Interference in the administration of electoral procedures is a critical concern. Partisan actors may attempt to manipulate aspects of the electoral process, such as voter registration, candidate nomination procedures, or the counting and verification of ballots.

7. Undermining the Independence of Electoral Management Bodies (EMBs): Efforts to undermine the independence of Electoral Management Bodies (EMBs) can compromise the impartial administration of elections. Partisan actors may attempt to exert influence over EMBs or question their credibility to cast doubt on election results.

8. Legal Maneuvering and Challenges: Partisan interference can extend to legal maneuvering, where political parties

exploit legal loopholes, file frivolous lawsuits, or challenge election results in an attempt to disrupt the electoral process or cast doubt on its legitimacy.

Partisan interference can be addressed or prevented by various means, such as revising or amending the electoral laws, clarifying or interpreting the electoral laws, harmonizing or coordinating the electoral laws, enforcing or applying the electoral laws, or challenging or litigating the electoral laws. However, addressing or preventing partisan interference can also face obstacles or resistance, such as political or economic interests, legal or technical complexities, or ethical or moral dilemmas. Therefore, addressing or preventing partisan interference requires careful analysis, consultation, and evaluation of the costs and benefits, as well as the potential risks and opportunities, of different options and alternatives.

Addressing the threat of partisan interference requires robust safeguards, transparent electoral processes, and vigilant oversight. Strengthening the independence of electoral institutions, promoting fair campaign financing practices, and fostering a culture of accountability are crucial steps in mitigating the impact of partisan interference on the impartial application of electoral laws.

Global Variances in Legal Frameworks

1. Comparative Analysis: Different Models, Shared Goals. A comparative analysis of legal frameworks across nations reveals diverse approaches to electoral legislation. Whether it's the first-past-the-post system or proportional representation, each model reflects a unique balance between stability and representation. Understanding these variations contributes to a nuanced perspective on the global landscape of democratic governance.

2. Challenges in Emerging Democracies. In nations navigating the path of democratization, establishing robust legal frameworks presents unique challenges. The delicate

balance between stability and inclusivity requires careful calibration, and the lessons learned from established democracies can inform the development of effective legal structures.

Electoral sanctity.

Electoral sanctity is the principle that elections should be free, fair and credible, and that the will of the people should be respected. There is no single global legal framework for electoral sanctity, but there are various international standards and guidelines that can help countries review and improve their electoral laws and regulations. Some of these are:

- International Electoral Standards: These are guidelines for reviewing the legal framework of elections, developed by the International Institute for Democracy and Electoral Assistance (IDEA). They cover topics such as electoral systems, electoral management bodies, voter registration, voting operations, counting and results, complaints and appeals, and electoral observation.

- International Obligations for Elections: These are guidelines for legal frameworks, developed by IDEA and the Office of the United Nations High Commissioner for Human Rights (OHCHR). They provide an inventory of United Nations jurisprudence relevant to electoral processes, such as human rights treaties, declarations, resolutions and recommendations.

- Legal Framework of Electoral Integrity: This is a topic on the ACE Electoral Knowledge Network, which provides information and resources on various aspects of electoral administration and reform. It explains the importance of the legal framework for protecting the integrity of elections, and provides examples of constitutions, laws and regulations from different countries and regions.

While there is no single, comprehensive global legal framework governing electoral sanctity, several international agreements, conventions, and principles contribute to the protection and promotion of fair, transparent, and democratic electoral processes. These instruments underscore the importance of free and fair elections as a fundamental component of democracy.

Global legal framework that address electoral sanctity:

1. Universal Declaration of Human Rights (UDHR):

The UDHR, adopted by the United Nations General Assembly in 1948, emphasizes the right to participate in government and to periodic and genuine elections that guarantee universal and equal suffrage. Articles 21 and 25 of the UDHR specifically address the right to take part in government and the right to vote in genuine elections.

2. International Covenant on Civil and Political Rights (ICCPR):

The ICCPR, adopted in 1966, further elaborates on the right to participate in government and the conduct of periodic, genuine elections. Article 25 of the ICCPR establishes the right of every citizen to take part in the conduct of public affairs, directly or through freely chosen representatives, and to vote and be elected.

3. International Foundation for Electoral Systems (IFES):

The IFES is a non-profit organization that provides assistance and support for elections worldwide. While not a legal framework in itself, the IFES promotes principles such as inclusiveness, transparency, and accountability in electoral processes. It offers resources and expertise to strengthen electoral systems globally.

4. Code of Conduct for International Election Observers:

The Code of Conduct for International Election Observers, adopted by the United Nations in 2005, outlines ethical standards for election observation missions. It emphasizes the importance of impartiality, objectivity, and respect for national laws to ensure the integrity of the electoral process.

5. African Charter on Democracy, Elections, and Governance:

The African Charter, adopted by the African Union in 2007, underscores the principles of democracy, the rule of law, and human rights. It emphasizes the holding of regular, free, and fair elections, as well as the peaceful transfer of power.

6. Declaration of Principles for International Election Observation:

This declaration, endorsed by several international organizations involved in election observation, outlines principles that guide the conduct of credible and impartial election observation. It emphasizes transparency, impartiality, and adherence to national laws.

7. Organization of American States (OAS) Electoral Observation Missions:

The OAS conducts election observation missions in the Americas and promotes electoral integrity. Its missions adhere to principles such as transparency, non-interference, and respect for national sovereignty.

8. Council of Europe's Venice Commission:

The Venice Commission provides legal assistance and advice on constitutional matters, including electoral laws. While not a binding legal framework, its guidelines and recommendations contribute to the development of fair and democratic electoral systems.

While these instruments and organizations contribute to the global legal framework for electoral sanctity, it's important to note that enforcement mechanisms vary, and adherence to these principles often relies on the commitment of individual states and the international community to uphold democratic values. Additionally, many countries have their own domestic legal frameworks that govern elections, further reinforcing the importance of a comprehensive approach to electoral sanctity.

Toward Strengthening Democratic Foundations

As we navigate the intricate tapestry of electoral legislations, recognizing both their historical roots and contemporary challenges, the imperative becomes clear: fortifying the legal foundations of democracy is essential in safeguarding against the tragedy of non-compliance. In the upcoming chapters, we will delve into strategies for reform and explore the intersection of legal frameworks with societal dynamics and media influences. Through this comprehensive lens, we aim to contribute to the ongoing dialogue on preserving the integrity of democratic processes.

Conclusion:

Challenges to free and fair elections in Africa: Elections are essential for democracy, but they also pose many challenges, especially in Africa, where many countries are still struggling with poverty, conflict, corruption, and poor governance. Some of the common challenges to free and fair elections in Africa include: logistical and technical difficulties, such as inadequate or faulty equipment, voter registration, and ballot distribution; security and violence, such as intimidation, harassment, or attacks on voters, candidates, or election officials; political and legal obstacles, such as lack of independence or impartiality of electoral institutions, manipulation or violation of electoral laws, and disputes or delays in resolving electoral complaints; and social and cultural factors, such as low voter education, civic engagement, or turnout, ethnic or religious polarization, or gender discrimination.

These challenges can undermine the credibility, legitimacy, and integrity of elections, and lead to public distrust, dissatisfaction, or protest Executive government interference: Executive government interference refers to the actions or influence of the incumbent president or government that affect the conduct or outcome of elections, often to their own advantage or benefit.

Executive government interference can take various forms, such as: abusing state resources, such as public funds, media, or security forces, to campaign or favor the ruling party or candidate; changing or ignoring constitutional or legal provisions, such as term limits, electoral boundaries, or voting rules, to extend or consolidate their power; restricting or repressing the opposition, civil society, or independent media, through harassment, arrest, censorship, or violence; or interfering or influencing the electoral management bodies, such as the electoral commission, the courts, or the observers, to compromise their autonomy, professionalism, or credibility. Executive government interference can distort the level playing field, undermine the democratic principles, and violate the human rights of elections, and lead to public resentment, resistance, or revolt.

The public trust challenge: The public trust challenge refers to the difficulty or necessity of building and maintaining the confidence and support of the public in the electoral process and its outcomes. Public trust is crucial for the success and sustainability of democracy, as it reflects the extent to which the people believe that their votes matter, that their voices are heard, and that their leaders are accountable.

Public trust can be enhanced or eroded by various factors, such as: the quality and performance of the electoral institutions, such as their transparency, accountability, or responsiveness; the behavior and attitude of the electoral stakeholders, such as their participation, cooperation, or acceptance; the information and communication of the electoral process, such as its accuracy, accessibility, or timeliness; and the context and environment of the electoral process, such as its stability, security, or development. Public trust can have various impacts on the electoral process, such as: increasing or decreasing voter turnout, engagement, or satisfaction; strengthening or weakening the legitimacy, credibility, or integrity of the electoral results; and promoting or preventing the peaceful resolution of electoral disputes or conflict.

In conclusion, the burden of trust placed on electoral umpires is immense, and the challenges faced in ensuring free and fair elections in Africa are deeply rooted. Acknowledging and addressing the interference by executive governments is crucial for upholding the principles of democracy. Furthermore, rebuilding and maintaining public trust necessitate transparency, inclusivity, and a commitment to rectifying past flaws. As African nations navigate these challenges, the lessons learned should inform the ongoing quest for fair, credible, and transparent electoral processes that truly reflect the will of the people.

CHAPTER 5

ELECTORAL GUIDELINES AND THE TRAGEDY OF NON-COMPLIANCE

"The health of a democratic society may be measured by the quality of functions performed by private citizens." – Alexis de Tocqueville

This chapter delves into the pivotal role of electoral guidelines and the consequences of non-compliance in the African electoral landscape. Examining issues such as public deception, umpire complicity, conflicts between laws and electoral guides, selective rules of engagement, and the shifting of goalposts by electoral umpires, this chapter sheds light on the complexities surrounding electoral processes in Africa.

5.1 Public Deception and Umpire Complicity

The intersection of public deception and umpire complicity poses a significant challenge to the integrity of elections.

This section explores instances where electoral umpires may inadvertently or knowingly contribute to public deception. It examines the role of misinformation, propaganda, and the manipulation of electoral guidelines, leading to a compromised electoral environment.

5.2 The Laws and Electoral Guide Impasse

Conflicts between existing laws and electoral guidelines can create confusion and undermine the legitimacy of electoral outcomes. This section dissects the challenges arising from discrepancies between legal frameworks and electoral guides. It analyzes the implications of such conflicts on the interpretation and application of electoral rules, potentially leading to contested results and diminished public trust.

5.3 The Tragedy of Selective Rules of Engagement

The selective application of rules during electoral processes introduces an element of bias and inconsistency. This section investigates situations where electoral umpires may apply guidelines selectively, favoring certain candidates or parties. It explores the consequences of such actions on the perceived fairness of elections and the overall trustworthiness of the electoral system.

5.4 How African Umpires Set Rules and Change the Goalpost Halfway

The dynamics of setting and altering rules mid-process can introduce unpredictability and undermine the credibility of elections. This section examines instances where electoral umpires set rules at the outset but later modify them during the electoral process. It explores the impact of such changes on the expectations of political actors, voters, and the legitimacy of the electoral outcome.

5.5 Lessons Learned:

Reflecting on past experiences provides valuable lessons for addressing challenges related to non-compliance with electoral guidelines. This section draws insights from both successful and flawed electoral processes, highlighting strategies employed to enhance compliance and rectify previous shortcomings. Lessons learned encompass the importance of clear communication, consistent application of rules, and measures to prevent public deception.

Non-compliance with electoral legislations can have significant societal repercussions, impacting the trust in the democratic process, social cohesion, and the overall health of a nation's governance. The consequences of such non-compliance may include:

1. Erosion of Trust in Democratic Institutions:

Non-compliance with electoral laws, such as instances of electoral fraud or manipulation, can erode public trust in democratic institutions. When citizens perceive that elections are not conducted fairly, it undermines their confidence in the legitimacy of elected leaders and the democratic system as a whole.

2. Political Polarization:

Non-compliance can exacerbate political polarization within society. Allegations of electoral misconduct or fraud may deepen existing divisions among political factions, leading to increased hostility, mistrust, and a breakdown in constructive political discourse.

3. Social Unrest and Protest:

Perceived non-compliance with electoral laws can trigger social unrest and protests. Citizens, frustrated by a lack of confidence in the electoral process, may take to the streets to express their grievances, demanding electoral justice and accountability.

4. Undermining Rule of Law:

Non-compliance with electoral legislations weakens the rule of law. When individuals or entities violate electoral laws with impunity, it sets a precedent that undermines the foundation of legal and democratic norms, risking a broader erosion of the rule of law in society.

5. Weakened Civic Engagement:

Lack of adherence to electoral laws may discourage civic engagement. If citizens perceive that their votes do not matter or that the electoral process is fundamentally flawed, they may become disillusioned and disengaged from participating in civic activities, including voting.

6. Ethnic or Social Division:

Non-compliance can contribute to or exacerbate existing ethnic or social divisions within a society. Manipulation of electoral processes may be perceived as favoring specific groups, leading to increased tension and discord along ethnic, religious, or social lines.

7. Economic Impact:

Political instability resulting from non-compliance can have economic consequences. Investors may be hesitant to commit resources to a politically uncertain environment, leading to a slowdown in economic development and growth.

8. International Relations and Reputation:

Non-compliance with electoral laws can negatively impact a country's international reputation. International observers, diplomatic partners, and the global community may scrutinize a nation's commitment to democratic principles, potentially resulting in strained diplomatic relations.

9. Loss of Legitimacy for Elected Leaders:

Leaders who emerge from elections tainted by non-compliance may face challenges in establishing legitimacy. Their ability to govern effectively and garner support may be compromised, hindering their capacity to address societal issues and implement policies.

10. Long-Term Democratic Backsliding:

Persistent non-compliance can contribute to long-term democratic backsliding. If electoral processes are consistently undermined, a nation may experience a gradual erosion of democratic institutions and principles, potentially leading to a more authoritarian style of governance.

Addressing non-compliance with electoral legislations requires a commitment to upholding the rule of law, ensuring transparent electoral processes, and holding accountable those who violate the established legal framework. Establishing and strengthening mechanisms for oversight, investigation, and legal consequences for electoral misconduct are crucial for preserving the integrity of democratic systems.

Non-compliance with electoral legislations is a serious issue that can undermine the integrity and legitimacy of elections, and have negative consequences for society. Some of the societal repercussions stemming from non-compliance with electoral legislations are:

- Loss of public trust and confidence in the electoral process and the institutions responsible for conducting and overseeing it. This can lead to apathy, disillusionment, or resentment among the voters and the candidates, and reduce their participation and representation in the political system.

- Erosion of the rule of law and the respect for human rights and fundamental freedoms. Non-compliance with electoral legislations can violate the rights of the voters and the candidates, such as the right to vote and to be elected, the right to a secret and equal ballot, the right to freedom of expression and association, and the right to a fair and effective remedy.

- Increase of social and political instability and conflict. Non-compliance with electoral legislations can create unfair advantages or disadvantages for certain parties or candidates, and distort the will of the people. This can trigger disputes, protests, violence, or even civil war, especially in fragile or divided societies.

- Impairment of social and economic development and progress. Non-compliance with electoral legislations can compromise the quality and accountability of governance, and enable corruption, fraud, or misuse of public resources. This can hinder the delivery of public services, the protection of the environment, and the promotion of human welfare.

These are some of the societal repercussions stemming from non-compliance with electoral legislations.

Erosion of Political Stability

1. Power Struggles and Instability

Non-compliance with electoral laws often triggers power struggles, creating a ripple effect of instability within the political arena. When the legitimacy of electoral outcomes is called into question, political entities engage in battles for recognition and control, fracturing the stability that is fundamental to effective governance.

2. Polarization and Divisiveness

The fallout from electoral non-compliance is frequently accompanied by increased polarization among citizens. The lines between political ideologies harden, fostering an 'us versus them' mentality. This divisiveness not only hampers constructive dialogue but also jeopardizes the collaborative spirit essential for the functioning of a healthy democracy.

Trust Deficits in Democratic Institutions

1. Citizen Distrust: A Harbinger of Democratic Erosion

The erosion of trust in democratic institutions is a telltale sign of the tragedy of non-compliance. When citizens lose confidence in the fairness of elections and the responsiveness of their representatives, the very foundations of democracy are shaken. Rebuilding this trust becomes imperative for the restoration of a resilient democratic society.

2. Impact on Civic Engagement

The health of a democracy is intricately tied to the level of civic engagement among its populace. Instances of non-compliance with electoral legislations can dampen civic enthusiasm, leading citizens to disengage from political processes out of disillusionment or a sense of futility. The consequences extend beyond the ballot box to impact broader civic responsibilities.

Economic Ramifications

1. Investor Confidence and Economic Stability

Political instability resulting from non-compliance has economic repercussions. Investors, seeking stable environments, may hesitate to engage with nations facing uncertain political landscapes. The link between political stability and economic prosperity underscores the interconnectedness of political and economic systems within a democratic framework.

2. Social Welfare Impacts

The effectiveness of governance, closely tied to electoral legitimacy, directly influences social welfare policies. When political instability prevails due to non-compliance, the formulation and execution of policies aimed at improving societal well-being may be hindered, exacerbating challenges faced by vulnerable populations.

Case Studies: Unpacking Societal Fallout

1. Latin American Democracies: Cycles of Instability

Examining instances in Latin America reveals cycles of political instability often rooted in contested electoral outcomes. Understanding these cases provides insights into how societal fallout can become entrenched, affecting not only political structures but also the daily lives of citizens.

2. African Nations: Striving for Stability

The challenges faced by some African nations in maintaining stable democracies illustrate the nuanced relationship between non-compliance, political stability, and societal well-being. By analyzing these cases, we gain a deeper understanding of the complex interplay of factors that contribute to the tragedy of democratic erosion.

Navigating the Aftermath

As we explore the intricate interplay between non-compliance with electoral laws and societal consequences, it becomes evident that the health of democracy is contingent on the resilience of its social fabric. The journey ahead involves not only addressing the immediate challenges posed by political instability but also fostering a renewed sense of civic responsibility and trust in the democratic process. In the chapters to come, we will delve into media influences and reform proposals aimed at mitigating the societal fallout of the tragedy weaved by non-compliance with electoral legislations.

Conclusion:

In conclusion, the tragedy of non-compliance with electoral guidelines in Africa is a multifaceted issue that demands careful scrutiny. Addressing public deception, umpire complicity, conflicts between laws and electoral guides, selective rules of engagement, and arbitrary rule changes is crucial for fostering trust in the electoral process. As African nations navigate these challenges, incorporating lessons learned from past experiences is essential for building resilient electoral systems that uphold the principles of democracy and truly reflect the will of the people.

CHAPTER 6

ELECTION RESULTS AND THE LEGITIMACY QUESTION

"When distant and unfamiliar and complex things are communicated to great masses of people, the truth suffers a considerable and often a radical distortion." – Walter Lippmann

Introduction:

Chapter 6 explores the aftermath of elections in Africa, focusing on the legitimacy question surrounding election results. It provides an overview of African elections, examines challenges to free and fair elections, analyzes the role of election petitions in addressing public trust issues, explores the divergence between voters' choices and declared results, and concludes with key lessons learned.

Section 6.1: African Elections Overview (200 words):

African elections encompass a diverse range of political systems, electoral processes, and historical contexts. Each country has its unique dynamics that shape the conduct and outcomes of elections. Some countries have made significant strides towards democratic governance, while others continue to face challenges. Understanding this diversity is crucial for contextualizing the issues surrounding the legitimacy of election results.

Section 6.2: Challenges to Free and Fair Elections (200 words):

Numerous challenges hinder the conduct of free and fair elections in Africa. These challenges include voter suppression, electoral violence, inadequate electoral infrastructure, and the manipulation of electoral laws. Voter suppression tactics, such as intimidation and voter registration obstacles, limit the ability of citizens to freely exercise their right to vote. Electoral violence, including conflicts and intimidation, undermines the peaceful conduct of elections. Inadequate electoral infrastructure, such as outdated voter registration systems and insufficient polling stations, hampers the efficiency and inclusivity of the electoral process. Manipulation of electoral laws, such as gerrymandering or biased media coverage, can distort the fairness of elections. Addressing these challenges is crucial to ensure transparent and unbiased elections.

Election Petitions and Public Trust Issues

Election petitions play a vital role in addressing concerns about the legitimacy of election results. These petitions provide a mechanism for citizens and political parties to challenge election outcomes and seek redress for perceived irregularities. They contribute to accountability and transparency in the electoral process. However, the handling of election petitions can significantly impact public trust. The timely resolution of petitions, impartiality of the judiciary, and adherence to due process are crucial for maintaining public confidence in the electoral process. Transparent and fair adjudication of election petitions helps address public trust issues and reinforces the legitimacy of election results.

Section 6.4: Voters' Choice and the Result Difference

An important aspect of the legitimacy question is the divergence between voters' choices and officially declared results. In some instances, the announced outcomes deviate from the expressed preferences of voters. Factors contributing to this difference include electoral fraud, voter manipulation, and lack of transparency in the vote-counting process. When voters' choices are not adequately reflected in the declared results, it erodes public trust and raises questions about the legitimacy of elected leaders. Ensuring that election results accurately reflect the will of the people is critical for upholding democracy and maintaining public confidence in the electoral process.

Section 6.5: Lessons Learned :

Reflecting on past elections provides valuable lessons for addressing the legitimacy question surrounding election results in Africa. Successful elections have demonstrated the importance of robust electoral institutions, transparent processes, and mechanisms for addressing grievances. Building strong electoral institutions that are independent, impartial, and well-resourced is essential for conducting credible elections. Transparency in the electoral process, including voter education, observation, and monitoring, helps foster trust and confidence. Additionally, establishing effective mechanisms for addressing electoral grievances, such as independent electoral commissions and impartial courts, allows for fair resolution of disputes and enhances the legitimacy of election outcomes.

The Media Landscape: A Double-Edged Sword

Media is a powerful and influential sphere that can shape public opinion, inform and educate voters, monitor and scrutinize electoral processes, and hold electoral actors accountable. However, media can also have a negative impact on the integrity and legitimacy of elections, if it is biased, inaccurate, or irresponsible.

1. The Fourth Estate: Guardian or Manipulator?

The media, often referred to as the Fourth Estate, is envisioned as a guardian of democracy, holding power accountable through unbiased reporting. However, the fine line between objective journalism and editorial influence can blur, opening avenues for the media to become a tool in the hands of those seeking to manipulate public opinion.

The Fourth Estate, traditionally defined as the media, plays a critical role in society by acting as a guardian of information and a watchdog over those in power. However, there are concerns about whether the media, in its various forms, functions as a guardian of truth and democracy or if it can be manipulated for various interests.

Historically, the Fourth Estate has been seen as a crucial component of a functioning democracy. It is expected to inform the public, hold those in power accountable, and provide a platform for diverse voices and opinions. A free and independent media is essential for citizens to make informed decisions and participate actively in democratic processes.

However, the media's role has been a subject of debate,

particularly in the context of sensationalism, bias, and the potential for manipulation. Some argue that media organizations, driven by commercial interests or political affiliations, may prioritize sensational stories over objective reporting. This sensationalism can distort the public's understanding of events and contribute to the spread of misinformation.

Bias in media coverage is another concern. Media outlets may be influenced by the political or economic interests of their owners or sponsors, leading to selective reporting or framing that aligns with particular ideologies. This bias can impact public perception and contribute to polarization within society.

Furthermore, the rise of digital media and social platforms has introduced new challenges. The speed at which information spreads on these platforms can outpace traditional fact-checking processes, leading to the rapid dissemination of misinformation or "fake news."

In some cases, media organizations themselves may be manipulated or coerced by external actors, including governments or powerful individuals, to disseminate specific narratives or suppress certain information. This manipulation can undermine the media's role as a guardian of truth and democracy.

Despite these challenges, many media organizations and journalists remain committed to journalistic ethics and principles. Investigative journalism, fact-checking initiatives, and efforts to promote media literacy are some ways in which the media seeks to fulfill its role as a guardian of information.

In conclusion, the Fourth Estate, while facing challenges and concerns about manipulation, remains a crucial pillar of democracy. The media's ability to provide accurate, unbiased information and hold power to account is essential for the functioning of democratic societies. Efforts to address issues of sensationalism, bias, and misinformation are vital in upholding the integrity of the Fourth Estate and ensuring its positive contribution to democratic governance.

2. Sensationalism and Clickbait: A Distortion of Reality

Sensationalism and clickbait are two phenomena in the media that contribute to a distortion of reality, often for the purpose of attracting attention and increasing viewership. While they may be effective strategies for capturing audience engagement, they also raise concerns about the accuracy and objectivity of information presented to the public.

In the digital age, the quest for higher ratings and increased online engagement has given rise to sensationalism and clickbait. The prioritization of attention-grabbing narratives over nuanced reporting can distort public understanding of electoral processes, contributing to the amplification of misinformation and polarization.

Sensationalism:

Sensationalism in the media involves the use of exaggerated, emotional, or shocking content to generate public interest and excitement. This can include focusing on the most sensational aspects of a story, emphasizing drama, and prioritizing entertainment value over informative value. Sensationalist reporting tends to elicit strong emotional reactions from the audience, but it may sacrifice accuracy and context in the process.

Clickbait:

Clickbait refers to online content, often in the form of headlines, thumbnails, or captions, designed to attract clicks and views. Clickbait typically relies on sensational language, intriguing questions, or provocative imagery to entice users to click on a link. The primary goal is to drive traffic to a website or platform, often for financial reasons, such as increasing advertising revenue. Clickbait can be misleading, as the actual content may not live up to the exaggerated promises made in the clickbait elements.

Distortion of Reality:

1. Selective Reporting: Sensationalism may lead to selective reporting, where media outlets prioritize sensational aspects of a story while neglecting more nuanced or essential information. This selective focus can distort the overall narrative and public perception.

2. Misrepresentation: Clickbait, with its enticing but exaggerated promises, can misrepresent the actual content.

Users who click on a sensationalized headline may find that the article or video does not deliver what was implied, leading to disappointment and a sense of manipulation.

3. Impact on Public Opinion: Sensationalism and clickbait can contribute to a distorted public understanding of events, issues, or individuals. The emphasis on sensational elements may overshadow critical details and nuances, leading to a polarized and incomplete view of reality.

4. Erosion of Trust: The use of sensationalism and clickbait can erode trust in media outlets. When audiences feel manipulated or misled, they may become skeptical of news sources, undermining the essential role of the media in informing the public.

Addressing sensationalism and clickbait requires media literacy education for consumers, ethical guidelines for content creators, and responsible editorial practices within media organizations. Balancing the need for audience engagement with a commitment to accuracy and context is crucial for maintaining the integrity of media in shaping public understanding of the world.

Media Narratives in the Face of Non-Compliance

1. Framing the Narrative: Influence on Public Perception

How the media frames narratives surrounding instances of non-compliance can significantly impact public perception. Whether highlighting irregularities or downplaying allegations, media outlets shape the lens through which citizens view the democratic process, influencing their trust in electoral outcomes.

2. Echo Chambers and Disinformation

The prevalence of echo chambers, where individuals are exposed primarily to information that aligns with their existing beliefs, exacerbates the challenge. Disinformation, intentionally false or misleading content, can thrive in these echo chambers, further deepening divisions and eroding confidence in the democratic system.

Media narratives play a significant role in shaping public perceptions, especially when it comes to issues of non-compliance. How the media frames and communicates stories related to non-compliance can influence public opinion, contribute to the understanding of the situation, and impact the way individuals and authorities respond. Here are some key points to consider:

Framing Non-Compliance:

1. Language and Tone: The language used by the media to describe non-compliance can influence how the audience perceives the situation. Terms like "protest," "resistance," "defiance," or "disobedience" carry different connotations and may shape public sympathy or disapproval.

2. Emphasis on Causes: Media narratives can focus on the underlying causes of non-compliance, providing context and helping the audience understand the motivations behind

certain actions. This can contribute to a more nuanced and empathetic public response.

Impact on Public Opinion:

1. Sympathy vs. Condemnation: The media's portrayal of individuals involved in non-compliance can sway public opinion. A sympathetic portrayal may garner support for the cause, while a condemnatory tone may lead to public disapproval.

2. Framing Solutions: Media narratives can also play a role in framing potential solutions to issues of non-compliance. Constructive reporting that highlights dialogue, negotiation, or policy changes can contribute to a more informed public discourse.

Government and Authority Responses:

1. Legitimacy and Accountability: The media can scrutinize government or authority responses to non-compliance, holding them accountable for their actions. The framing of official responses can impact perceptions of the legitimacy of measures taken.

2. Humanizing vs. Demonizing: The media's portrayal of individuals involved in non-compliance, as well as law enforcement or authorities, can humanize or demonize different parties. This framing influences how the public views the actions taken by both sides.

Media Responsibility and Objectivity:

1. Balanced Reporting: Responsible journalism aims for

balanced reporting that presents multiple perspectives on non-compliance. Providing a comprehensive view of the situation allows the audience to form more informed opinions.

2. Avoiding Sensationalism: Media narratives should strive to avoid sensationalism that could distort the reality of non-compliance events. Responsible reporting includes fact-checking, verification of sources, and presenting information in a contextually accurate manner.

3. Ethical Considerations: Journalistic ethics play a crucial role. Media outlets should consider the potential impact of their narratives on social cohesion, public safety, and democratic processes, balancing the need for transparency with ethical reporting practices.

In summary, media narratives have the power to shape public understanding of non-compliance. The framing, language, and emphasis in reporting can influence public opinion, government responses, and the overall discourse surrounding issues of disobedience or resistance. Responsible and ethical journalism is essential for fostering an informed and engaged public.

International Perspectives on Media Influence

1. Comparative Analysis: Diverse Approaches

A comparative analysis of media landscapes across nations reveals diverse approaches to reporting on electoral matters. Understanding these differences provides insights into the varying degrees of media influence on shaping public perceptions of non-compliance and its consequences.

2. Media Freedom and Accountability

The level of media freedom within a nation is a critical factor in assessing the potential impact of media on democratic processes. Striking a balance between media freedom and accountability becomes paramount to ensure that journalistic principles align with the responsibility of safeguarding democratic values.

Media can help promote compliance with electoral legislations by raising awareness and understanding of the legal framework of elections, such as the rules and procedures for conducting elections, resolving disputes, and ensuring accountability. Media can also report on the implementation and enforcement of the electoral laws, and expose any violations or irregularities that may occur. Media can also provide a platform for dialogue and debate among electoral stakeholders, and facilitate the participation and representation of diverse voices and interests.

Media can also contribute to non-compliance with electoral legislations by spreading misinformation or propaganda, inciting violence or intimidation, or favoring or discriminating against certain parties or candidates. Media can also violate the electoral laws, such as the regulations on media access, coverage, and advertising, or the provisions on secrecy and equality of the ballot. Media can also undermine the credibility and authority of the electoral authorities, courts, or observers, and challenge or reject the electoral results.

Media can also be affected by non-compliance with electoral legislations by other actors, such as political parties, candidates, or state officials. Media can face harassment, threats, or attacks for reporting on electoral issues, or be denied access to information or sources. Media can also be subjected to censorship, interference, or manipulation by the state or other powerful interests, or be influenced by corruption, fraud, or pressure. Media can also be constrained by legal loopholes, weak institutions, or lack of oversight.

Case Studies: Media's Role in Shaping Political Narratives

1. United States: Polarization and Partisan Media

Exploring the media landscape in the United States unveils the challenges posed by partisan news outlets and the polarization of political discourse. The impact of media narratives on electoral trust provides valuable insights into the complexities of media influence within established democracies.

2. Russia: State-Controlled Narratives

Examining the media landscape in Russia highlights the implications of state-controlled narratives on public perceptions of electoral processes. Understanding how media influences operate in contexts where press freedom is restricted offers crucial perspectives on the global dynamics of media and democracy.

Striking a Balance: Responsible Journalism and Public Awareness

1. Media Literacy Initiatives

Fostering media literacy among citizens becomes a vital component of mitigating the negative impact of media on democratic processes. Educating the public on discerning credible sources and understanding media biases equips individuals to navigate the complexities of information dissemination.

2. Ethical Journalism and Accountability

Media organizations play a pivotal role in upholding democratic values through ethical journalism practices. Establishing and adhering to codes of conduct that prioritize accuracy, fairness, and accountability is essential in fostering a media landscape that strengthens, rather than weakens, democratic institutions.

The Road Ahead: A Call for Media Responsibility

The role and performance of the Fourth Estate are influenced by various factors, such as the economic and technological forces that are transforming the news media, the political and social forces that are challenging or threatening the news media, and the legal and ethical forces that are regulating or guiding the news media. The Fourth Estate faces many challenges and opportunities in the modern world, and needs constant vigilance and improvement to ensure its quality and legitimacy.

As we navigate the intricate interplay between media and the tragedy of non-compliance with electoral legislations, the imperative for responsible journalism becomes clear. In the chapters to come, we will explore reform proposals aimed at enhancing media integrity and promoting public awareness. By addressing the challenges within the media landscape, we strive to contribute to the resilience of democracy in the face of evolving threats.

Conclusion :

The legitimacy of election results is crucial for democratic governance in Africa. Addressing challenges to free and fair elections, ensuring the integrity of the electoral process, and bridging the gap between voters' choices and declared results are essential for building resilient electoral systems. By incorporating lessons learned from past experiences, such as strengthening electoral institutions, promoting transparency, and providing avenues for addressing grievances, African nations can foster a democratic landscape that commands public trust and reflects the true will of the people.

Chapter 6 also delved into the influential sphere of media and its profound impact on the tragedy of non-compliance with electoral legislations. As a powerful disseminator of information, the media shapes public perceptions, frames political narratives, and plays a pivotal role in either upholding or undermining the integrity of the democratic process.

CHAPTER 7

LAWS AND THE BENCH PREDICAMENT

"The secret of change is to focus all of your energy, not on fighting the old, but on building the new." – Socrates

Electoral fraud is a serious issue that undermines the legitimacy and integrity of democratic elections. It refers to any illegal or unethical interference with the process or outcome of an election, such as vote rigging, ballot stuffing, voter intimidation, or suppression1. Electoral fraud can have various motives and consequences, such as maintaining or gaining political power, influencing public policies, or eroding public trust in democracy.

Poor legislations are one of the factors that can facilitate or encourage electoral fraud. Poor legislations can be defined as laws or regulations that are vague, inconsistent, outdated, or inadequate to address the challenges and complexities of modern elections. Poor legislations can create loopholes or ambiguities that can be exploited by fraudsters, or create barriers or burdens that can discourage or disenfranchise legitimate voters.

Some examples of poor legislations that can contribute to electoral fraud are:

Lack of clear and comprehensive rules for voter registration, identification, and verification, which can allow ineligible or duplicate voters to cast ballots, or prevent eligible voters from exercising their right to vote.

Lack of effective and transparent mechanisms for ballot security, counting, and auditing, which can enable tampering, manipulation, or misreporting of votes.

Lack of adequate and consistent regulations for campaign finance, media access, and political advertising, which can create unfair advantages or disadvantages for certain candidates or parties, or misinform or mislead voters.

Lack of independent and impartial electoral management bodies, judicial institutions, and oversight agencies, which can compromise the credibility and accountability of the electoral process, or fail to prevent, detect, or prosecute electoral fraud.

To prevent or reduce electoral fraud, it is essential to have sound and robust legislations that can ensure the integrity, transparency, and fairness of the electoral process. Such legislations should be based on international standards and best practices, and reflect the specific needs and context of each country. Moreover, legislations should be regularly reviewed and updated to address emerging challenges and opportunities, such as new technologies, social media, or civic engagement.

Electoral fraud is not only a legal or technical problem, but also a political and social one. Therefore, legislations alone are not sufficient to combat electoral fraud. It also requires the active participation and cooperation of all stakeholders, including political parties, candidates, voters, civil society, media, and international observers, to uphold the values and principles of democracy, and to respect the will of the people.

This chapter delves into the intricate relationship between legal frameworks, the judicial system, and the electoral process in Africa. Focusing on the challenges posed by poor legislations, the role of the African legal community in handling election matters, and the impact of judicial decisions on democratic governance, this chapter navigates the complex terrain of laws and the bench predicament.

7.1 Poor Legislations: An Aide Memoire to Electoral Fraud

The foundation of a robust electoral system lies in well-crafted legislations. This section examines instances of poor legislation that serve as vulnerabilities, potentially facilitating electoral fraud. It explores how inadequacies in electoral laws can undermine the integrity of the democratic process, providing an unintended aide-memoire for those seeking to manipulate elections.

7.2 The African Bar Approach to Election Matters

The role of legal professionals, particularly the African bar, in shaping the electoral landscape is pivotal. This part of the chapter investigates how legal practitioners engage with election matters. It explores the strategies employed by lawyers in advocating for fair electoral processes, addressing legal loopholes, and safeguarding the principles of democracy.

7.3 African Democracy and the Tale of Judicial

Emasculation

The judiciary plays a crucial role in upholding the rule of law and ensuring the integrity of elections. This section scrutinizes instances where the judiciary faces challenges, both external and internal, leading to its perceived emasculation. It explores how external pressures, political interference, or internal conflicts can compromise the independence and effectiveness of the judiciary in the context of elections.

7.4 Fundamental Rights and State Interest Limitations

The delicate balance between individual rights and state interests shapes the legal framework surrounding elections. This section analyzes the interplay between fundamental rights, such as the right to vote, and the limitations imposed by state interests. It explores how these dynamics influence electoral laws and court decisions, emphasizing the need for a judicious balance.

7.5 Lessons Learned:

Examining past legal challenges and judicial decisions provides valuable lessons for navigating the bench predicament. This section draws insights from cases where legal frameworks were strengthened, judicial independence was preserved, and the rule of law prevailed. Lessons learned encompass the importance of legal advocacy, the protection of fundamental rights, and the resilience of legal institutions in the face of external pressures.

7.6 Conclusion:

In conclusion, the intricate dance between laws and the bench in African democracies underscores the need for a robust legal framework and an independent judiciary. As the continent grapples with the challenges posed by poor legislations, the role of the African bar, the potential emasculation of the judiciary, and the delicate balance between rights and state interests, lessons learned from past experiences should guide the ongoing efforts to fortify the legal foundations of democracy. The conclusion reflects on the imperative of legal resilience, the protection of democratic values, and the continuous pursuit of justice in electoral processes.

Poor Legislations: An Aide-Memoire to Electoral Fraud

In the intricate tapestry of democratic governance, the strength of electoral systems is intricately woven into the quality of legislations that underpin them. This section delves into the perilous realm of poor legislations, serving as an unwitting aide-memoire that echoes the vulnerabilities and susceptibilities leading to electoral fraud in African democracies.

1. The Pervasiveness of Electoral Fraud:

Before dissecting the role of poor legislations, it is essential to acknowledge the persistent challenge of electoral fraud. From voter suppression to ballot manipulation, electoral fraud threatens the very essence of democratic ideals. Understanding its multifaceted nature is crucial to appreciating the role of legislative deficiencies.

2. Poor Legislations as Vulnerabilities:

The legislative framework surrounding elections should act as a fortress against fraudulent activities. However, when legislations are poorly crafted, they inadvertently become open windows through which malfeasance can enter. These vulnerabilities may include ambiguous language, inadequate safeguards, or legislative gaps that ill-intentioned actors exploit.

3. Ambiguities and Interpretation Challenges:

One of the hallmarks of poor legislations is ambiguity. This section explores how vague language or poorly defined procedures create room for interpretation challenges. The lack of clarity may allow for manipulation by those seeking to exploit legislative gaps to their advantage.

4. Inadequate Safeguards and Oversight:

An effective legislative framework should incorporate robust safeguards and oversight mechanisms. Poor legislations, however, often lack these critical components. The absence of checks and balances provides fertile ground for fraudulent practices, as the electoral process operates without the necessary scrutiny and accountability.

5. Legislative Gaps and Exploitation:

Legislative gaps act as catalysts for electoral fraud. This section examines instances where inadequate laws fail to cover emerging challenges or evolving forms of malpractice. These gaps create opportunities for exploitation, enabling individuals or groups to engage in activities that fall outside the purview of existing legislations.

6. Implications for Democratic Integrity:

The ramifications of poor legislations reverberate throughout the democratic system. The compromised integrity of elections erodes public trust, undermines the legitimacy of elected leaders, and fosters a climate of disillusionment among citizens. The fragility introduced by legislative shortcomings poses a substantial threat to the democratic edifice.

7. Addressing Poor Legislations:

Recognizing the menace posed by poor legislations is the first step toward mitigating electoral fraud. This section explores potential strategies for addressing legislative deficiencies, including comprehensive legislative reviews, stakeholder consultations, and the incorporation of international best practices to fortify electoral frameworks.

8. Lessons Learned and the Path Forward:

Understanding the impact of poor legislations on electoral fraud provides invaluable lessons. This section reflects on past experiences, emphasizing the need for proactive legislative reforms, public awareness campaigns, and the cultivation of a culture that values the integrity of the democratic process.

In conclusion, poor legislations act as an inadvertent aide-memoire to electoral fraud, leaving an indelible mark on the democratic landscape. Recognizing, addressing, and learning from these deficiencies are essential steps in fortifying the foundations of democracy and ensuring that the voice of the people is authentically heard through the electoral process.

The African Bar Approach to Election Matters

The legal fraternity, often referred to as the "African Bar," plays a pivotal role in shaping and safeguarding democratic processes across the continent. This section explores the distinctive approach taken by African legal professionals in handling election matters, highlighting their strategies, challenges, and contributions to the advancement of democratic governance.

1. Legal Advocacy for Electoral Integrity:

The African Bar serves as a vanguard for electoral integrity, employing legal advocacy to uphold the principles of fair and transparent elections. This involves legal professionals actively engaging with electoral laws, scrutinizing their implementation, and challenging any infringements that may compromise the democratic process.

2. Safeguarding Legal Frameworks:

Ensuring the robustness of electoral laws is paramount for the African Bar. Legal professionals work diligently to identify loopholes, inconsistencies, and inadequacies within existing legislations. They contribute to the reform and enhancement of legal frameworks to address emerging challenges and promote the integrity of the electoral system.

3. Defending Electoral Justice:

The African Bar is at the forefront of defending electoral justice. Legal professionals take on crucial roles in representing aggrieved parties, filing election petitions, and navigating the intricacies of the judicial process. Their commitment to upholding the rule of law contributes to the resolution of disputes and the restoration of public trust in the electoral outcome.

4. International Collaboration and Best Practices:

Recognizing the interconnected nature of democratic governance, the African Bar actively engages in international collaboration. Legal professionals leverage global best practices, draw insights from successful electoral models, and participate in forums that facilitate the exchange of knowledge. This collaborative approach enhances the capacity of the African legal community to address common challenges and adopt effective strategies.

5. Challenges Faced by the African Bar:

Despite their crucial role, legal professionals within the African Bar encounter various challenges. These may include political pressure, threats to personal safety, and institutional constraints. Navigating these challenges requires resilience, courage, and a steadfast commitment to the principles of justice and democracy.

6. Public Education and Awareness:

The African Bar recognizes the importance of public education in fostering a culture of legal literacy and civic engagement. Legal professionals actively contribute to initiatives that educate the public on their rights, the electoral process, and the role of the legal system in ensuring accountability and transparency.

7. Contributions to Electoral Reforms:

The African Bar is instrumental in advocating for and contributing to electoral reforms. Legal professionals engage with policymakers, electoral bodies, and civil society to influence positive changes in electoral laws and procedures. Their expertise enriches the discourse on legal reforms, aiming for a more resilient and accountable democratic framework.

8. Lessons Learned:

This section reflects on the experiences and lessons learned by the African Bar in handling election matters. It explores instances of successful legal interventions, collaborative efforts, and the impact of legal strategies on electoral outcomes. These lessons inform future approaches to continually strengthen the role of the legal community in advancing democracy.

9. Conclusion:

In conclusion, the African Bar's approach to election matters is characterized by a commitment to justice, the rule of law, and the enhancement of democratic processes. As legal professionals navigate challenges, collaborate internationally, and contribute to electoral reforms, they play a crucial role in shaping the trajectory of democratic governance in Africa. The collective efforts of the African Bar contribute to the resilience and credibility of electoral systems, fostering a democratic landscape that reflects the will of the people.

Pillars of Democracy

The pillars of democracy are the essentials of every democratic government and where those pillars are absent, the government may not be able to function properly. In light of the above, here are the 10 pillars of democracy. Pillars that holds democracy from falling

Below are the 10 major pillars of democracy:

1. Legitimacy

Legitimacy simply means the acceptance and recognition of the power to govern given to the leaders. It is one of the major pillars of democracy because the absence of legitimacy means that the people did not legally assign political powers to their leaders to govern them.

Legitimacy cannot be achieved when there is no periodical elections, conducted to enable the people appoint their leaders. It should also be noted that the same way the people can legitimately appoint their leaders, they can also legitimately remove whoever they want from power through impeachment or recall.

2. Separation of powers

Separation of powers is another important pillar of democracy. It is the segmentation of government powers to sidestep the problem of dictatorship and tyrannical leadership. Usually, the segment of powers is between the legislature, executive and judicial pillars of the government.

So, instead of bestowing all political powers on one person of group of people or allowing just one arm of government to perform all government functions, powers and functions will be shared between the arms.

In most cases, the legislature will perform the law making function, the judiciary will perform the interpretation function and the executive will execute the law.

3. Popular participation

Democracy is unlike a monarchy where only persons from the lineage of the king or queen can rule. It is a system where everyone leads either directly or through representatives.

For this reason, opinion polls and consultations are regular activities when political decisions are to be taken in a democratic nation. Thorough research and debating are usually done within government representatives before government policies are reached or executed.

An example of a country where this is seen is the Nigeria. Before the government takes any political move there is usually a deliberation of it in the National Assembly at the federal level and the various States House of Assemblies to ensure that it is for the best interest of the people.

4. Periodic elections

This pillar means that the people have the right to choose their leaders and representatives through periodic and genuine elections. It also means that the elections are conducted in a transparent, impartial, and accountable manner, and that the results reflect the will of the people. Through period elections democracy is able to avoid dictatorship by leaders. When leaders are conscious of the fact that they were elected by the people and that they will leave office after certain period, they will be forced to act in accordance with the law and respect for the people's interest.

Periodic elections is one of the tenets of democracy that cannot be overlooked. It is very important because it is the key pillar of democracy and also an important feature of a democratic system as well.

Think about it this way; a nation that claims to be practicing democracy cannot be said to be a true democratic nation if there is no period election. The essence of democracy is to avoid arbitrary rules and one of the way to ensure that is through periodic elections.

5. Checks and balances

Checks and balances is a political theory and a very essential pillar of government. This theory posits that there should be a mutual oversight and limitation by the arms of government in order to prevent abuse of power. We have already explained how separation of powers helps to foster democracy and fight against dictatorship in government. Now, the theory of checks of balances further helps to achieve that by allowing the arms of government to check the activities of each other.

Another reason for the theory of checks and balances is to curb excesses of power by one arm of the government. Thus, the judiciary can check the activities of the legislature or executive to see whether they are both acting under their assigned constitutional powers. In turn, the legislature can check the activities of others and the executive can also do the same.

6. Rule of law

Rule of law simply means supremacy of the law. It posits that the law is above everybody in a political system and thus, no arm of government, agency or organization is supreme. This pillar means that everyone is equal before the law and that the law is applied fairly and consistently. It also means that the law protects the rights and freedoms of the people and limits the power of the government.

The theory of rule of law was propounded by A.V Dicey. It is one of the greatest features and tenets of democracy because the dreams and aspirants of the people are contained in the law. This therefore makes the law Supreme even above the government itself.

It should be noted however that there are many factors that can actually limit the rule of law in a nation. Some of them includes: immunity of leaders, etc.

7. Fundamental human rights

The last important pillar of democracy is fundamental human rights. These rights are free given rights which are inalienable and immutable. Fundamental human rights are seen as one of the pillars of democracy because they protect the interest of citizens. Take for instance, the Universal declaration of human right ensures that member countries provide for the fundamental human rights of their citizens by entrenching it in the constitution. These rights includes the right to life, right to freedom of speech, right to freedom of expression, freedom of movement etc. Where these rights are not provided for in the constitution, then there is no true democracy because the interest of the people are not well protected.

8. Accountability and Transparency: A successful democracy is built on the fundamental foundations of transparency and accountability. Transparency assures that public and media access, as well as public knowledge of government acts, decisions, and procedures. It indicates that people have a right to know what their government is up to and how it is utilising the commons.

On the other hand, accountability refers to holding individuals in authority accountable for their deeds and choices. It includes procedures for holding those responsible for wrongdoing, corruption, or abuse of authority accountable. A few examples of accountability procedures are audits, inquiries, and legal action.

Transparency and accountability go hand in hand in a democratic society to thwart corruption, preserve public confidence, and guarantee that elected officials and public workers behave in the best interests of the people.

9. Civil Society and NGOs (Non-Governmental Organizations): A strong democracy needs both an active civil society and the presence of NGOs. The term "civil society" refers to a broad spectrum of nonprofit organisations, activist groups, and associations established by private persons.

Particularly in tackling diverse social, political, and environmental challenges, NGOs are extremely important.

These groups give people a forum on which to express their worries, fight for their rights, and hold the government responsible. They frequently operate as a conduit between citizens and decision-makers, bridging the gap between societal demands and governmental responses.

NGOs and civil society organisations can carry out tasks including research, awareness-building, protest planning, and social service delivery. They support civic involvement, monitor human rights, and participate in policy deliberations.

By doing this, they contribute to ensuring that individuals have access to means of participating in democracy and influencing governmental choices.

10. The Constitution is a major pillar of democracy because it is the fundamental law that defines and regulates the political system and the rights and duties of the citizens. The Constitution establishes the basic principles and values of democracy, such as the sovereignty of the people, the rule of law, the separation of powers, the protection of human rights, and the participation of the public in the governance process. The Constitution also sets the limits and checks and balances of the power of the government and its institutions, and provides the mechanisms and procedures for conducting free and fair elections, resolving electoral disputes, and ensuring electoral accountability. The Constitution also reflects the history, culture, and aspirations of the people, and can be amended or reformed to adapt to the changing circumstances and needs of the society.

The Constitution is therefore a vital pillar of democracy, as it lays the foundation and framework for the democratic system and process, and safeguards the rights and interests of the people. Without a Constitution, or with a Constitution that is weak, vague, or violated, the democracy may not function properly or may be threatened by dictatorship, corruption, or violence.

Constitution

The constitution is the fundamental laws, rules, regulations and other related elements according to which democratic state are expected to be governed. It can also be defined as a book or document that contains the rules and principles by which a state is governed. It is a body of fundamental principles or established precedents according to which a state or other organization is acknowledged to be governed. The constitution of a country dictates how power is shared among the arms of Government and the rights and duties of citizens in the country

Sources of constitution

The main sources of Nigerian Constitution include the following:

1. History of the people

2. Decrees

3. Convention

4. The custom of the people

5. Acts of parliament

Constitution as a major pillar of democracy

Constitutions can be regarded as a pillar of democracy because of the following functions its performs in a country

1. It sets the limit of power of the use of powers of Government

2. It protects the right of the minority

3. The constitution defines the right and power of

Government

4. It helps to share power among the arms of Government

5. It also spelt out political institution, party system, tenure of office of Government, etc.

6. The constitution protects the right of the minority

7. It reflects the sovereign will of the people.

8. Lays down of the aims, objectives, values and goals which the people want to secure.

9. It contains a description and guarantee of the fundamental rights of the people.

10. It gives a detailed account of the organization of the government. The organization, powers and functions of its three organs of government and their interrelationship.

11. In a federation, the Constitution lays down the division of powers between the central government and the governments of the federating states/provinces. It is binding upon both the centre and the state governments.

12. It specifies the power and method of amendment of the Constitution.

13. The constitution governs all and no one can violate its rules.

14. It lays down the election system

15. It provides for the independence of judiciary and rule of law

There is no definitive or universal list of the pillars of democracy, as different sources and scholars may have different views on what constitutes the essential principles and institutions that support and sustain democratic governance.

- Protection of human rights: This pillar means that the people have the right to enjoy their basic rights and liberties, such as the right to life, liberty, and security, the right to freedom of expression and association, and the right to participate in public affairs. It also means that the government respects and protects these rights and does not violate or abuse them. [13]

- Civil society: This pillar refers to the voluntary associations and organizations that operate outside the state and the market, such as NGOs, trade unions, religious groups, and social movements. Civil society can enhance democracy by promoting civic engagement, social capital, pluralism, and accountability.

- Media: This pillar refers to the various channels and platforms of communication and information, such as newspapers, radio, television, and the internet. Media can support democracy by informing and educating the public, monitoring and scrutinizing the electoral process, and providing a space for public debate and participation.

- Education: This pillar refers to the process and system of learning and teaching, both formal and informal, that shapes the knowledge, skills, and values of the people. Education can foster democracy by developing critical thinking, civic awareness, and democratic culture among the citizens.

- Accountability: This pillar means that the government and its officials are answerable and responsible to the people for their actions and performance. It also means that the people have the right and the means to oversee, evaluate, and sanction the government and its officials.

- Transparency: This pillar means that the government and its officials operate in an open and clear manner, and that the people have the right and the access to information about the government and its activities. It also means that the government and its officials disclose and justify their decisions and actions to the public.

- Responsiveness: This pillar means that the government and its officials listen and respond to the needs, demands, and preferences of the people. It also means that the government and its officials adapt and adjust their policies and programs to reflect the changing circumstances and expectations of the people.

Disregard for electoral laws can undermine the democratic system by violating or weakening some of these pillars of democracy. For example:

- Disregard for electoral laws can erode the rule of law and the protection of human rights, by allowing the government or other actors to manipulate, interfere, or rig the electoral process, and by denying or restricting the rights of the voters and the candidates, such as the right to vote and to be elected, the right to a secret and equal ballot, the right to freedom of expression and association, and the right to a fair and effective remedy.

- Disregard for electoral laws can compromise the free and fair elections and the separation of powers, by creating unfair advantages or disadvantages for certain parties or candidates, and by distorting the will of the people. This can undermine the legitimacy and the accountability of the government and its officials, and reduce their responsiveness to the public interest.

- Disregard for electoral laws can impair the civil society and the media, by limiting or suppressing their role and influence in the electoral process. This can reduce the civic engagement, social capital, pluralism, and accountability of the democracy, and weaken the public debate and participation.

- Disregard for electoral laws can hinder the education and the transparency of the democracy, by preventing or obscuring the public access to information and knowledge about the electoral process and its outcomes. This can affect the critical thinking, civic awareness, and democratic culture of the citizens, and make them more vulnerable to misinformation or propaganda.

These are some of the ways that disregard for electoral laws can undermine the democratic system and its pillars.

As Mark Twain once quipped, "History doesn't repeat itself, but it often rhymes." Through case studies and anecdotes, we draw parallels between historical events and current affairs, seeking to discern the patterns that threaten the very essence of democratic governance.

Our exploration extends to the legal frameworks that serve as the backbone of electoral processes. Eleanor Roosevelt's words, "Justice cannot be for one side alone, but must be for both," remind us of the need for fairness in the formulation and enforcement of electoral laws. We assess the strengths and vulnerabilities of these frameworks, proposing reforms that aspire to fortify the foundations of democracy.

The societal fallout from non-compliance is profound, impacting not only the political landscape but also the social fabric of communities. Alexis de Tocqueville's observation that "The health of a democratic society may be measured by the quality of functions performed by private citizens" becomes a lens through which we scrutinize the consequences of non-compliance on civic engagement and public trust.

Media, with its transformative power to shape perceptions, occupies a central role in our analysis. Walter Lippmann's assertion that "When distant and unfamiliar and complex things are communicated to great masses of people, the truth suffers a considerable and often a radical distortion" prompts us to scrutinize the responsibility of media in fostering an informed citizenry.

These are some of the essential reform proposals aimed at fortifying the pillars of democracy against the tragedy of non-compliance with electoral legislations.

Enhancing Legal Frameworks

1. Closing Legal Loopholes

Addressing vulnerabilities within electoral laws requires a comprehensive review to identify and close loopholes. Legislative bodies should collaborate with legal experts and civil society to draft amendments that strengthen the legal framework, leaving minimal room for exploitation.

2. Independent Electoral Commissions

Establishing independent electoral commissions with broad representation can bolster the fairness of elections. These bodies should be insulated from political interference, ensuring their impartiality in overseeing electoral processes, enforcing regulations, and adjudicating disputes.

Fostering Inclusivity and Representation

1. Electoral Reforms for Inclusive Participation

Introducing electoral reforms that prioritize inclusivity is crucial. Measures such as proportional representation, gender quotas, and measures to address socio-economic disparities can contribute to a more representative and diverse political landscape.

2. Civic Education Initiatives

Educating citizens on the importance of participation and the mechanics of the democratic process is fundamental. Civic education initiatives, integrated into school curricula and public awareness campaigns, empower individuals to make informed choices and engage meaningfully in civic life.

Media Integrity and Responsibility

1. Media Ethics and Standards

Strengthening media integrity requires the establishment and enforcement of ethical standards. Media organizations should adhere to transparent codes of conduct, emphasizing accuracy, fairness, and the responsibility to provide unbiased information to the public.

2. Media Literacy Programs

Media literacy programs should be widely implemented to equip citizens with the skills needed to critically evaluate information sources. By fostering an understanding of media biases and manipulation techniques, these programs empower individuals to navigate the complex media landscape.

Technological Safeguards

1. Cybersecurity Measures

Given the digital evolution of electoral processes, implementing robust cybersecurity measures is imperative.

Electoral authorities should collaborate with cybersecurity experts to safeguard voting systems, voter databases, and communication channels from cyber threats.

2. Transparent Technology Adoption

The adoption of new technologies should prioritize transparency. Open-source software, verifiable paper trails, and audit mechanisms can enhance the accountability of digital voting systems, providing citizens with confidence in the reliability of electoral outcomes.

Strengthening International Cooperation

1. Election Monitoring and Diplomacy

International organizations and diplomatic efforts play a crucial role in upholding democratic values globally. Strengthening election monitoring mechanisms and fostering diplomatic initiatives to address electoral challenges can contribute to a shared commitment to democratic principles.

2. Knowledge Sharing and Capacity Building

Facilitating knowledge sharing among nations facing similar challenges fosters a collaborative approach to strengthening democracy. Capacity-building programs can assist emerging democracies in developing resilient institutions and navigating the complexities of electoral governance.

Public Engagement and Accountability

1. Transparency in Campaign Financing

Promoting transparency in campaign financing is vital to

preventing undue influence. Implementing strict disclosure requirements and monitoring mechanisms can curtail the potential for financial interests to manipulate the electoral process.

2. Citizen Oversight and Accountability Mechanisms

Empowering citizens to actively participate in oversight is essential. Establishing citizen-driven oversight mechanisms, such as independent watchdog groups and ombudsman offices, enhances accountability and fosters public trust in the democratic process.

Building a Culture of Democracy

1. Civic Dialogues and Inclusive Decision-Making

Encouraging civic dialogues and inclusive decision-making processes cultivates a culture of democracy. Engaging citizens in meaningful discussions on policy issues and involving diverse voices in decision-making contribute to a sense of ownership and collective responsibility.

2. Long-Term Civic Engagement Programs

Long-term civic engagement programs, including community forums, town halls, and grassroots initiatives, nurture an ongoing commitment to democratic values. These programs foster a sense of civic duty, encouraging citizens to actively participate beyond electoral cycles.

The Collective Imperative

As we delve into reform proposals, it becomes clear that

safeguarding democracy is a collective imperative. By focusing our energy on building resilient systems, we shift the narrative from the tragedy of non-compliance to a vision of democratic governance strengthened by transparency, inclusivity, and civic engagement. In the chapters that follow, we will explore the international perspective on non-compliance, drawing lessons from global experiences and examining the potential for collaborative efforts to fortify the pillars of democracy.

CHAPTER 8

VOTER'S AWARENESS AND THE FALLACY OF PUBLIC PARTICIPATION

"In the long history of the world, only a few generations have been granted the role of defending freedom in its hour of maximum danger." – John F. Kennedy

This chapter delves into the critical relationship between voter awareness, public participation, and the broader dynamics of democracy in Africa. It explores the challenges faced by African voters in accessing information, the consequences of poor government attention to civic rights, issues of public contempt, and the nexus between public awareness and political violence.

8.1 How African Voters Are Left Uninformed:

Access to accurate and comprehensive information is fundamental to informed decision-making in a democracy. This section investigates the challenges faced by African voters in obtaining reliable information about candidates, policies, and electoral processes. It explores factors such as media restrictions, limited educational resources, and information asymmetry that contribute to voters being left uninformed.

8.2 Poor Government Attention to Civic Rights:

The commitment of governments to fostering an informed electorate is crucial. This part of the chapter examines instances where governments in Africa fall short in prioritizing civic rights and providing the necessary resources for civic education. The lack of emphasis on cultivating an engaged and knowledgeable citizenry contributes to the fallacy of public participation.

8.3 Public Contempt and Issues of Civil Disobedience:

A lack of awareness and perceived disregard for civic rights can lead to public contempt and, in extreme cases, civil disobedience. This section explores how disenfranchised and uninformed voters may express their discontent through various forms of civil disobedience, jeopardizing the stability of democratic institutions.

8.4 Public Awareness and the Political Violence Nexus:

The nexus between public awareness and political violence is a complex and concerning aspect of democracy in Africa. This part of the chapter investigates how a lack of awareness can contribute to the manipulation of public sentiments, exacerbate political tensions, and escalate into acts of violence. It emphasizes the role of public awareness as a mitigating factor in curbing political violence.

8.5 Lessons Learned:

Drawing lessons from instances where voter awareness has been compromised, this section reflects on the consequences of an uninformed electorate. It explores successful strategies employed in different contexts to enhance voter awareness and civic education, highlighting the importance of empowering citizens with knowledge to strengthen democratic processes.

8.6 Conclusion:

In conclusion, the fallacy of public participation, stemming from insufficient voter awareness, poses significant challenges to the democratic fabric in Africa. As the continent grapples with these issues, it is imperative to recognize the importance of investing in civic education, fostering governmental commitment to civic rights, and addressing the nexus between public awareness and political violence. The conclusion emphasizes the lessons learned and the need for concerted efforts to ensure that African voters are not left uninformed but, instead, are empowered to actively participate in shaping the democratic landscape.

Case Studies: Lessons Learned

1. Brazil: Populism and Democratic Erosion

Examining the Brazilian experience sheds light on the challenges posed by populist leaders and the erosion of democratic norms. Understanding the complex interplay of political, social, and economic factors offers valuable lessons for nations grappling with similar challenges.

2. South Africa: Transitioning to Democracy

South Africa's transition from apartheid to democracy presents a positive example of overcoming historical injustices. However, the post-apartheid era has faced challenges related to corruption and governance, highlighting the ongoing work required to strengthen democratic institutions.

International Cooperation: A Collective Response

1. United Nations and Democratic Governance

The United Nations plays a crucial role in promoting democratic governance globally. Through initiatives like the Sustainable Development Goals (SDGs), the UN emphasizes the importance of inclusive, accountable, and transparent institutions as essential components of sustainable development.

2. Diplomatic Alliances and Solidarity

Diplomatic alliances among like-minded nations provide a platform for collective action. By fostering solidarity and sharing best practices, nations can build a united front against the erosion of democratic values and actively support one another in times of crisis.

Strengthening International Norms

1. Norms Against Electoral Interference

The establishment of international norms condemning electoral interference is essential. By collectively denouncing actions that undermine the integrity of electoral processes, nations can contribute to a shared commitment to upholding democratic principles on the global stage.

2. Election Observation and Assistance

International organizations, such as the Organization for Security and Co-operation in Europe (OSCE), play a vital role in election observation and assistance. Their presence helps ensure that electoral processes adhere to international standards, fostering transparency and accountability.

Building a Resilient Global Democracy

1. Global Citizenship and Responsibility

Promoting a sense of global citizenship and responsibility is integral to the defense of democracy. Recognizing that the health of democratic institutions worldwide is interconnected underscores the importance of individuals, communities, and nations actively contributing to the preservation of democratic values.

2. Learning from Shared Histories

Learning from shared histories, both successes and failures, enhances the global community's collective resilience. By drawing on the experiences of nations that have successfully navigated challenges or rebounded from setbacks, the international community can build a repository of knowledge to confront future threats.

Africa: Non-compliance of electoral laws can be caused by various factors, such as weak institutions, lack of resources, political interference, corruption, violence, or external pressure. Non-compliance of electoral laws can also lead to various problems, such as disputed results, electoral fraud, human rights violations, social unrest, or civil war. Some of the examples of non-compliance of electoral laws in Africa include the postponement of elections in Somalia and Ethiopia, the repression of opposition in Uganda and Tanzania, and the brutality of security forces in Kenya and

South Africa.

Asia: Non-compliance of electoral laws can be influenced by various factors, such as cultural diversity, religious extremism, military intervention, authoritarianism, or populism. Non-compliance of electoral laws can also result in various issues, such as electoral manipulation, human rights abuses, social polarization, or political instability. Some of the examples of non-compliance of electoral laws in Asia include the military coup in Myanmar, the crackdown on dissent in Hong Kong, and the violence and fraud in Afghanistan and Pakistan.

Europe: Non-compliance of electoral laws can be driven by various factors, such as nationalism, populism, corruption, or foreign interference. Non-compliance of electoral laws can also create various challenges, such as electoral irregularities, human rights infringements, social division, or democratic backsliding. Some of the examples of non-compliance of electoral laws in Europe include the disputed referendum in Catalonia, the constitutional crisis in Poland, and the allegations of Russian meddling in the UK and France.

These are some of the global perspectives on non-compliance of electoral laws.

Conclusion: A Call to Collective Action

As we conclude this exploration of global perspectives on the tragedy of non-compliance with electoral legislations, the call to collective action resounds. In an interconnected world, where the fate of democracies is intertwined, the defense of freedom and democratic values becomes a shared responsibility. By learning from one another, fostering international cooperation, and actively participating in the global dialogue on democracy, nations can stand united against the shadows that threaten the pillars of democratic governance.

CHAPTER 9

CIVIL SOCIETY AND FOREIGN INTERESTS; A TALE OF INDIFFERENCE

"Democracy must be built through open societies that share information. When there is information, there is enlightenment. When there is debate, there are solutions. When there is no sharing of power, no rule of law, no accountability, there is abuse, corruption, subjugation, and indignation." – Atifete Jahjaga

This chapter delves into the intricate relationship between civil society, foreign interests, and the challenges faced by African democracies. It explores the role of foreign observers, the struggles of black democracies to establish themselves, changes in the landscape of civil society organizations, and the lessons drawn from this complex interplay.

9.1 The Role of Foreign Observers in African Democracies:

Foreign observers play a significant role in monitoring and evaluating elections in African democracies. This section examines the contributions, limitations, and potential biases associated with the presence of foreign observers. It considers how their involvement impacts the perception of electoral processes and the broader democratic landscape.

9.2 Why Black Democracies Struggle to Stand:

The struggle for stable and enduring democracies in African nations is a complex narrative. This part of the chapter analyzes historical, socio-economic, and geopolitical factors that contribute to the challenges faced by black democracies in establishing themselves. It explores issues such as institutional fragility, external influences, and post-colonial legacies.

9.3 Many Civil Society Organizations; What Has Changed?

Civil society organizations (CSOs) play a crucial role in advocating for democratic values. This section investigates the changing dynamics within civil society in Africa. It explores whether the proliferation of CSOs has translated into more effective advocacy, increased civic engagement, and tangible improvements in the democratic landscape.

9.4 Lessons Learned:

Examining the experiences of civil society and foreign interests in African democracies provides valuable lessons. This section reflects on instances where foreign involvement has positively contributed to democratic development and where it may have inadvertently perpetuated challenges. It also considers the evolution of civil society and the effectiveness of their efforts in promoting democratic values.

9.5 Conclusion:

In conclusion, the tale of indifference between civil society, foreign interests, and African democracies is a multifaceted narrative that requires nuanced understanding. While foreign observers and civil society can contribute positively to democratic development, challenges and potential pitfalls exist. The conclusion emphasizes the need for a balanced and informed approach to foreign involvement, the imperative of addressing internal challenges faced by black democracies, and the continuous evolution of civil society in adapting to the changing dynamics of democratic governance. Lessons learned should guide future efforts to foster resilient, self-sustaining democracies that genuinely reflect the aspirations of the people.

Chapter 9 navigates the path toward democratic resilience, drawing on the lessons gleaned from the preceding chapters and offering a roadmap for nations seeking to fortify their democratic foundations. In the face of challenges posed by non-compliance with electoral legislations, this chapter explores strategies for building resilient democracies that endure and flourish.

Democracy is witnessing a global decline, as revealed by the latest Democracy Index 2016 from the Economist Intelligence Unit (EIU). In the past year, 72 countries experienced a deterioration in democratic values, outnumbering those showing improvement by more than 2 to 1.

The EIU's Democracy Index evaluates the state of democracy by assessing electoral processes, pluralism, civil liberties, government functionality, political participation, and political culture in over 160 countries. The average global democracy score in 2016 dropped to 5.52 from 5.55 in 2015 on a scale of 0 to 10.

Norway leads the world as the strongest democracy, followed by Iceland, Sweden, New Zealand, Denmark, and joint sixth-place holders Canada and Ireland. Switzerland, Finland, and Australia complete the top ten "full democracies."

The report highlights that less than half (49%) of the world's population resides in some form of democracy, with only

4.5% in a "full democracy," marking a substantial decline from just under 9% in 2015.

The significant decline is primarily attributed to the United States being reclassified as a "flawed democracy" due to low public confidence in the government, a trend evident before the election of President Donald Trump. Similar patterns were observed in several other developed economies.

The question arises about the democratic nature of the United Nations (UN), particularly considering the structure of the Security Council, which holds more power and influence than other UN organs. This prompts discussions on the fairness and democratic nature of the Security Council, given its 15-member composition, including five permanent members with veto power.

Arguments supporting the UN as a democratic institution emphasize its principle of sovereign equality among its 193 member states, providing a platform for global dialogue and cooperation. The UN actively promotes democracy, human rights, and good governance worldwide through various organs and agencies, with the Security Council deemed necessary for maintaining international peace and security.

Contrarily, critics argue that the UN is undemocratic, dominated by powerful and wealthy nations, failing to represent the diverse needs of the majority. Allegations include the UN's inability to uphold and enforce democratic principles globally due to political deadlock, bureaucratic inefficiency, or resource limitations. The Security Council is particularly scrutinized for its exclusive and unaccountable nature, accused of advancing its interests and interfering in the internal affairs of other countries, undermining the views of the broader UN membership.

Human factor in upholding electoral integrity

The Human Factor plays a crucial role in upholding or undermining electoral integrity. Individuals, including politicians, election officials, voters, and other stakeholders, can significantly impact the fairness, transparency, and legitimacy of electoral processes. Here are some key aspects related to the Human Factor in the context of electoral integrity:

A. Exploration of the role of individuals in upholding or undermining electoral integrity:

- Politicians and Candidates: Political leaders and candidates have a responsibility to uphold electoral integrity by promoting fair competition, refraining from engaging in corrupt practices, and respecting democratic norms. Their actions and statements can influence public trust in the electoral process.

- Election Officials: The conduct of election officials, such as electoral commissions, administrators, and personnel involved in the administration of elections, is crucial. They should act impartially, ensure transparency in the electoral process, and enforce electoral laws and regulations.

- Voters: Individual voters can uphold electoral integrity by exercising their right to vote freely and fairly, without coercion or manipulation. Their informed choices contribute to the legitimacy of electoral outcomes.

B. Case studies on prominent figures influencing electoral compliance:

Examining case studies of prominent figures can provide insights into how individuals can influence electoral compliance, both positively and negatively. These case studies can include examples of politicians who have championed electoral integrity, election officials who have demonstrated integrity in their roles, as well as instances of individuals who have undermined electoral processes through corruption, voter suppression, or disinformation campaigns.

C. Public accountability and ethical consideration:

Public accountability is essential for upholding electoral integrity. Individuals involved in the electoral process, including politicians and election officials, should be accountable for their actions and decisions. Mechanisms such as transparency in campaign financing, public disclosure of conflicts of interest, and independent oversight bodies can enhance accountability.

Ethical considerations are also crucial. Individuals should adhere to ethical standards, including honesty, fairness, and respect for democratic values. They should prioritize the public interest over personal or partisan gains, avoid spreading misinformation or engaging in disinformation campaigns, and maintain the confidentiality and security of electoral data.

Promoting public accountability and ethical considerations can be achieved through mechanisms such as codes of conduct for politicians and election officials, civic education campaigns on electoral ethics, and independent monitoring of electoral processes.

Overall, the Human Factor plays a significant role in the upholding or undermining of electoral integrity. By focusing on the actions and behaviors of individuals, addressing issues of accountability, and promoting ethical considerations, electoral systems can be strengthened, public trust can be enhanced, and the integrity of democratic processes can be safeguarded.

Indeed, in-depth case studies can provide valuable insights into the behavior and strategies of prominent figures who have influenced electoral compliance, shedding light on patterns that either strengthen or undermine the foundations of free and fair elections. Analyzing these case studies can offer important lessons for safeguarding electoral integrity. Here are some key points in this regard: ·

1. Political Leaders:

- Examination of political leaders can reveal how their actions and rhetoric impact electoral compliance. Some leaders may prioritize democratic principles, promote transparency, and respect the rule of law, thus strengthening electoral integrity. Others may engage in tactics that undermine the fairness and legitimacy of elections, such as voter suppression, manipulation of electoral laws, or using inflammatory language that fuels polarization and undermines public trust.

- Case studies can highlight the importance of leaders who actively promote electoral integrity, foster dialogue and inclusivity, and ensure that electoral laws and regulations are followed. Their strategies can serve as examples for creating an environment conducive to free and fair elections.

2. Election Officials:

- The behavior and decisions of election officials significantly influence electoral compliance. Case studies can examine instances where election officials have demonstrated impartiality, transparency, and integrity in their roles, effectively upholding electoral standards and ensuring fair processes.

- Conversely, case studies can also shed light on situations where election officials have succumbed to political pressure, engaged in corrupt practices, or failed to enforce electoral laws adequately. Understanding these patterns can inform efforts to strengthen the independence and professionalism of electoral management bodies.

3. Influential Personalities:

- Prominent individuals, such as media personalities, social media influencers, or public figures, can exert significant influence over public opinion and electoral processes. Case studies can reveal how these personalities leverage their platforms to either support or undermine electoral integrity.

- By examining the strategies and tactics employed by influential figures, lessons can be learned about the impact of disinformation campaigns, hate speech, or manipulative messaging on electoral outcomes. This understanding can guide efforts to counteract these negative influences and promote a more informed and responsible public discourse.

Overall, in-depth case studies provide a rich source of information on how prominent figures influence electoral compliance. By analyzing their behavior, strategies, and tactics, valuable lessons can be gleaned for safeguarding electoral integrity. These lessons can inform the development of policies, reforms, and initiatives aimed at creating an environment that upholds the principles of free and fair elections, strengthens democratic institutions, and fosters public trust.

Strengthening Democratic Institutions

1. Institutional Independence and Robust Oversight

Ensuring the independence of key institutions, including electoral commissions, judiciaries, and oversight bodies, is paramount. Robust oversight mechanisms, both domestic and international, contribute to accountability and safeguard the integrity of democratic processes.

2. Constitutional Safeguards

Constitutional safeguards play a pivotal role in upholding democratic principles. Nations should continually assess and reinforce constitutional provisions that protect the rule of law, individual rights, and the separation of powers, creating a resilient framework resistant to erosion.

Civic Empowerment and Participation

1. Civic Education and Media Literacy

Empowering citizens through civic education and media literacy programs fosters an informed and engaged electorate. Equipping individuals with the skills to critically evaluate information and actively participate in civic life enhances the resilience of democratic societies.

2. Inclusive Decision-Making

Promoting inclusive decision-making processes ensures that diverse voices are heard. Civic dialogues, participatory governance, and mechanisms for citizen input contribute to a sense of ownership and strengthen the social fabric of democracy.

Adapting to Technological Challenges

1. Cybersecurity and Electoral Integrity

As technology evolves, prioritizing cybersecurity in electoral processes becomes imperative. Regular assessments, updates, and international cooperation on cybersecurity measures safeguard voting systems from external threats, preserving the sanctity of elections.

2. Ethical Technology Adoption

Adopting technology ethically and transparently is essential. Nations should consider the societal impact of technological advancements, ensuring that digital tools enhance democratic processes without compromising fairness, transparency, or privacy.

Ethical technology adoption refers to the responsible and conscientious integration of technology into various aspects of society, organizations, and individual lives, considering the ethical implications and consequences of such adoption. This involves making informed and morally sound decisions about the development, deployment, and use of technology to ensure that it aligns with ethical principles, values, and societal well-being. Here are key considerations for ethical technology adoption:

1. Privacy Protection: Respect for individuals' privacy is paramount. Ethical technology adoption involves implementing robust privacy measures, obtaining informed consent, and safeguarding personal data from unauthorized access or misuse.

2. Transparency and Accountability: Organizations should be transparent about how they collect, use, and share data. They must also be accountable for the consequences of their technological implementations, taking responsibility for any negative impacts on individuals or society.

3. Fairness and Equity: Ensure that technology is designed and deployed in a way that avoids reinforcing existing biases and discrimination. Ethical adoption requires promoting fairness and equity, especially in algorithms and artificial intelligence systems.

4. Inclusivity and Accessibility: Consider the needs of diverse user groups to create inclusive technologies. Efforts should be made to ensure accessibility for individuals with disabilities, bridging the digital divide, and making technology available to everyone.

5. Security and Cybersecurity: Ethical technology adoption involves prioritizing security to protect against cyber threats and ensure the safety of users. Robust cybersecurity measures are essential to prevent data breaches and

unauthorized access.

6. Environmental Impact: Assess and minimize the environmental impact of technology adoption. This includes considerations such as energy efficiency, responsible e-waste management, and the overall sustainability of technological systems.

7. User Empowerment: Empower users by providing them with control over their data, preferences, and interactions with technology. Ethical adoption encourages user autonomy and informed decision-making.

8. Ethical AI and Automation: When deploying artificial intelligence and automation, ensure that these systems adhere to ethical guidelines. This includes transparency in decision-making processes and addressing concerns related to job displacement.

9. Public Engagement and Consultation: Involve the public in decision-making processes related to technology adoption, particularly in areas that significantly impact society. Public consultation helps incorporate diverse perspectives and ensures democratic decision-making.

10. Continuous Ethical Review: Regularly review and reassess the ethical implications of technology use. As technology evolves, ethical considerations may change, requiring ongoing evaluation and adaptation of policies and practices.

11. Global Responsibility: Consider the global implications

of technology adoption. Ethical considerations should extend beyond local contexts to address potential impacts on a global scale, particularly in the interconnected digital world.

By prioritizing ethical considerations in technology adoption, individuals, organizations, and policymakers contribute to building a more responsible, inclusive, and sustainable technological landscape.

International Collaboration

1. Diplomatic Alliances and Solidarity

Diplomatic alliances among nations committed to democratic values provide a foundation for solidarity. Through shared initiatives, joint diplomatic efforts, and collective responses to challenges, nations can amplify their impact in defending democracy on the global stage.

2. Global Norms and Standards

Establishing and reinforcing global norms and standards against electoral interference and democratic erosion creates a united front. The international community can work collaboratively to set expectations for adherence to democratic principles and hold those deviating accountable.

Continuous Adaptation and Learning

1. Institutional Resilience through Reform

Institutions should embrace a culture of continuous reform. Regular assessments, adaptive measures, and a commitment to learning from both successes and setbacks contribute to institutional resilience and the ability to withstand evolving challenges.

2. Knowledge Exchange and Peer Learning

Facilitating knowledge exchange and peer learning among nations fosters a dynamic approach to democratic governance. Sharing best practices, strategies, and lessons learned creates a supportive environment where nations can collectively navigate the complexities of maintaining resilient democracies.

Conclusion: A Call to Sustained Action

As we conclude this journey toward democratic resilience, the call to sustained action echoes. Building and maintaining resilient democracies require ongoing dedication, collaboration, and a commitment to the principles that underpin democratic governance. In the face of challenges posed by non-compliance with electoral legislations, nations stand united in the shared pursuit of enduring freedom, accountability, and the empowerment of their citizens. The roadmap outlined in this chapter serves as a guide, inviting nations to embark on a collective journey toward a future where democracy not only survives but thrives.

CHAPTER 10

MILITARY INCURSIONS AND THE DOCTRINE OF NECESSITY

"The best way to predict the future is to create it." – Peter Drucker

This chapter delves into the complex intersection of military incursions, the doctrine of necessity, and the historical context of African democracies. It explores the consequences of democratic failures, the dynamics of strong economies under military regimes, the perception of military interregnum as a necessary evil, fallacies associated with democracy, and lessons drawn from the historical transitions in countries such as Ghana and Nigeria.

10.1 If Democracy Fails, What Next?:

This section delves into the critical question of what unfolds when democratic governance faces significant challenges or outright failure. It explores the circumstances that may lead to military interventions, examining the factors that are perceived as threats to the stability and functionality of democratic systems.

10.2 Strong Economies Under the Military Regime:

Contrary to the assumption that military rule inevitably leads to economic decline, this part of the chapter investigates instances where military regimes have presided over strong economies. It explores the factors that contribute to economic stability under military governance, examining both the positive and negative aspects of such regimes.

10.3 Military Interregnum; A Necessary Evil:

The concept of military interregnum as a necessary evil is

explored in this section. It analyzes the circumstances under which military interventions are deemed necessary for restoring order, addressing governance challenges, and implementing reforms. The ethical and practical implications of such interventions are considered within the broader context of democratic governance.

10.4 Fallacies of Democracy and the Military Respite:

Examining perceived fallacies of democracy, this section explores the narrative that military rule can provide a respite from the challenges associated with democratic governance. It delves into the arguments presented by proponents of military interventions and the contrasting view that such interventions may compromise long-term democratic values.

10.5 Military Transitions History and the Ghana/Nigeria Example:

This part of the chapter delves into the historical transitions between military and civilian rule, focusing on the examples of Ghana and Nigeria. It explores the patterns, challenges, and outcomes of transitions between military and civilian governance in these countries, providing insights into the broader dynamics of political change.

10.6 Lessons Learned:

Drawing lessons from historical and contemporary military interventions, this section reflects on the complexities and consequences associated with such transitions. It considers the impact on democratic institutions, societal trust, and the challenges of rebuilding democratic governance after periods of military rule.

10.7 Conclusion:

In conclusion, the intricate relationship between military incursions, the doctrine of necessity, and the historical transitions in African democracies presents a nuanced narrative. The chapter emphasizes the need for a thorough understanding of the factors that contribute to democratic challenges, the implications of military interventions, and the importance of learning from historical examples. As African nations navigate the complexities of governance, the lessons drawn from military transitions should inform efforts to build resilient democratic systems that can withstand internal challenges and external pressures.

CHAPTER 11

REGIONAL BLOCKS AND DIPLOMATIC LIMITATIONS

"Democracy is not just a political system; it is a way of life, an individual and collective journey towards freedom, equality, and justice." – Unknown

This chapter explores the intricate dynamics between regional blocks, diplomatic protocols, and the challenges faced by African democracies. It delves into the delicate balance between state sovereignty and external intervention, the protocols governing diplomatic involvement, global limitations on democracy, the influence of regional blocks, and the effectiveness of organizations such as the African Union (AU) and ECOWAS.

11.1 Diplomatic Protocols and Intervention Dilemma:

Regional Blocks and Diplomatic Limitations

The interaction between regional blocks and diplomatic considerations is a nuanced aspect of international relations, especially in the context of African democracies. This chapter delves into the complexities surrounding regional blocks and the limitations they face in influencing diplomatic affairs within their respective spheres.

1. The Significance of Regional Blocks:

Before dissecting the limitations, it is essential to recognize the importance of regional blocks in fostering cooperation, economic integration, and political collaboration among neighboring nations. This section briefly outlines the functions and goals of regional blocks, emphasizing their role in regional stability and development.

2. Diplomatic Protocols and Sovereignty Concerns:

One of the primary limitations faced by regional blocks lies in the delicate balance between diplomatic protocols and concerns about state sovereignty. Regional bodies must navigate the fine line between respecting the autonomy of member states and addressing collective challenges that may warrant diplomatic intervention.

3. Internal Strife and Non-Interference Principles:

Internal conflicts within member states pose a significant challenge to regional blocks. The principle of non-interference in the internal affairs of member nations, while crucial for respecting sovereignty, can limit the ability of regional bodies to address issues such as human rights violations, political instability, or democratic deficits.

4. Economic Interests vs. Political Objectives:

Regional blocks often comprise nations with diverse economic interests and political objectives. Balancing these varied interests becomes a limitation when pursuing cohesive diplomatic strategies. Economic considerations may sometimes take precedence over political imperatives, impacting the effectiveness of regional diplomatic efforts.

5. Inadequate Institutional Capacity:

Limited institutional capacity within regional bodies can hinder diplomatic initiatives. Insufficient resources, organizational structures, and decision-making mechanisms may impede the timely and effective response of regional blocks to diplomatic challenges, including those related to democracy and governance.

6. Power Dynamics and Hegemony:

Power dynamics among member states within a regional block can further complicate diplomatic endeavors. Hegemonic influences or power imbalances may create divisions and prevent unified diplomatic action, especially when addressing sensitive political issues.

7. Varied Democratic Standards:

The existence of varied democratic standards among member states introduces diplomatic challenges. Regional blocks may grapple with reconciling different levels of democratic maturity, making it challenging to adopt a uniform approach in addressing democratic deficits within the region.

8. External Influences and Global Dynamics:

The influence of external actors and global dynamics poses external limitations on regional blocks. Interactions with major global players, such as superpowers or international organizations, can shape the diplomatic landscape and affect the autonomy of regional blocks in addressing regional democratic challenges.

9. Lessons from Past Diplomatic Engagements:

Drawing insights from historical and contemporary diplomatic engagements, this section reflects on the lessons learned. It examines instances where regional blocks navigated limitations successfully and identifies areas for improvement in diplomatic strategies.

10. Future Prospects and Recommendations:

Looking forward, this part of the chapter explores potential avenues for overcoming diplomatic limitations. It considers strategies for enhancing institutional capacity, fostering greater unity among member states, and adapting diplomatic approaches to meet the evolving challenges faced by regional blocks.

11. Conclusion:

In conclusion, the chapter underscores the intricate dynamics between regional blocks and diplomatic limitations in the context of African democracies. It emphasizes the need for strategic diplomacy, institutional strengthening, and a collective commitment to overcome challenges. As regional blocks continue to play a crucial role in shaping diplomatic engagements, understanding and addressing these limitations are imperative for fostering regional stability and promoting democratic values.

This section navigates the complex landscape of diplomatic protocols and the dilemmas associated with intervention. It analyzes the ethical considerations, international norms, and diplomatic challenges that arise when regional blocks contemplate intervening in the affairs of sovereign nations to address democratic deficits or political crises.

11.2 State's Sovereignty and Allied Limitations on Democracy:

Diplomatic Protocols and Intervention Dilemma:

The delicate interplay between diplomatic protocols and the dilemma of intervention represents a complex challenge in international relations. This section delves into the nuanced dynamics of diplomatic engagements, exploring the protocols that guide such interactions and the intricate dilemmas faced when contemplating intervention in the affairs of sovereign nations.

1. The Framework of Diplomatic Protocols:

Diplomatic protocols serve as the backbone of international relations, providing a structured framework for communication, negotiation, and collaboration between nations. This subsection outlines the fundamental principles that govern diplomatic engagements, emphasizing the importance of sovereign equality, non-interference, and respect for state sovereignty.

2. The Ethical Dilemma of Intervention:

The heart of the intervention dilemma lies in the ethical considerations surrounding the decision to interfere in the internal affairs of a sovereign nation. This part of the section explores the moral and ethical dimensions that diplomats and international actors grapple with when faced with situations that demand intervention to address issues such as human rights abuses, political instability, or democratic deficits.

3. Criteria for Intervention: Balancing Act:

Navigating the intervention dilemma requires a careful balancing act. This subsection outlines the criteria often considered when contemplating intervention, including the severity of the situation, the urgency of action, and the legitimacy of the cause. It delves into the complexities of defining clear criteria and the challenges associated with making ethically sound decisions.

4. The United Nations and International Law:

The role of the United Nations and international law in shaping diplomatic protocols and intervention is paramount. This section explores the mechanisms within the UN framework that provide a legal basis for intervention, examining the Security Council's authority and the responsibility to protect (R2P) doctrine.

5. Challenges to Diplomatic Protocols:

While diplomatic protocols aim to provide a structured approach to international relations, various challenges can hinder their effective implementation. This part of the section highlights challenges such as the lack of consensus among nations, differing interpretations of international law, and the potential for powerful nations to influence diplomatic outcomes.

6. The Humanitarian Imperative:

One of the driving forces behind intervention is the humanitarian imperative. This subsection discusses how the desire to prevent or alleviate human suffering often clashes with diplomatic protocols that emphasize non-interference. It explores cases where the urgency of humanitarian crises has led to a reevaluation of traditional diplomatic norms.

7. The Role of Regional Organizations:

Regional organizations play a crucial role in navigating the intervention dilemma. This part of the section examines how regional bodies can act within diplomatic protocols to address crises in their spheres of influence. It discusses the challenges and opportunities presented by regional intervention, emphasizing the need for a coordinated approach with global diplomatic norms.

8. Lessons from Historical Interventions:

Drawing insights from historical interventions, this subsection reflects on the lessons learned. It analyzes cases where diplomatic protocols were tested, intervention occurred, and the outcomes shaped future approaches. The examination of successes and failures informs contemporary diplomatic strategies.

9. Conclusion: Striking a Balance:

In conclusion, the section underscores the complexity of the intervention dilemma within the framework of diplomatic protocols. It emphasizes the ongoing challenge of striking a balance between respecting state sovereignty and fulfilling the moral imperative to protect human rights. As the international community grapples with evolving crises, the chapter calls for a nuanced approach that acknowledges the complexities of intervention while upholding the principles of diplomacy and international law.

Examining the principle of state sovereignty, this part of the chapter explores how the concept, while crucial for international relations, can present limitations on efforts to promote and strengthen democracy. It addresses the delicate balance between respecting a nation's sovereignty and the collective responsibility to uphold democratic values.

11.3 Protocols on Intervention and Interference Diplomacy:

Protocols on Intervention and Interference Diplomacy:

Navigating the intricate landscape of international relations, this section explores the protocols that guide diplomatic interventions and the complexities associated with interference diplomacy. It delves into the principles, challenges, and ethical considerations surrounding interventions in the affairs of sovereign nations.

1. Principles Governing Intervention:

At the core of diplomatic protocols on intervention lies a set of principles designed to uphold international order and protect common values. This subsection outlines these principles, including the respect for state sovereignty, the responsibility to protect (R2P), and the promotion of human rights. It highlights the delicate balance required to adhere to these principles while addressing pressing global issues.

2. Legitimate Grounds for Intervention:

Identifying legitimate grounds for intervention remains a challenge in diplomatic practice. This part of the section explores situations where the international community deems intervention justifiable, such as cases of genocide, crimes against humanity, or threats to regional stability. It scrutinizes the criteria that define legitimate grounds and the complexities associated with their interpretation.

3. The Role of International Organizations:

International organizations play a pivotal role in framing and implementing protocols on intervention. The subsection examines how bodies like the United Nations (UN) contribute to establishing norms for diplomatic intervention. It also discusses the challenges faced by these organizations in reaching consensus and executing effective interventions.

4. Sovereignty Concerns and Non-Interference:

One of the primary dilemmas in interference diplomacy is the tension between the imperative to intervene and the principles of state sovereignty and non-interference. This section explores how diplomatic protocols grapple with the need to address global challenges while respecting the autonomy of nations. It considers the ethical implications of balancing sovereignty concerns with the responsibility to protect.

5. Challenges in Defining Intervention:

Defining the scope and nature of intervention remains an ongoing challenge in diplomatic discourse. This part of the section analyzes the difficulties associated with delineating the boundaries of interference diplomacy, taking into account cultural, political, and contextual variations that impact perceptions of intervention.

6. Ethics of Intervention: Striking the Right Balance:

Ethical considerations play a crucial role in shaping protocols on intervention. This subsection delves into the ethical dilemmas faced by diplomats and international actors, emphasizing the importance of striking the right balance between intervention and non-interference to ensure that actions align with global moral standards.

7. Humanitarian Intervention: A Contested Concept:

Humanitarian intervention, a subset of diplomatic interference, often sparks debates on its legitimacy. This part of the section examines the contested nature of humanitarian intervention, exploring instances where it has been invoked, the challenges faced in its application, and the ongoing discourse surrounding its ethical implications.

8. Regional Approaches to Intervention:

Regional bodies also contribute to the discourse on intervention. This subsection explores how regional organizations develop their protocols, addressing crises within their spheres of influence. It considers the advantages and challenges of regional approaches to intervention and their coordination with broader international norms.

9. Lessons from Historical Interventions:

Drawing insights from historical interventions, this part of the section reflects on the lessons learned. It analyzes cases where diplomatic protocols were tested, intervention occurred, and the outcomes shaped future approaches. The examination of successes and failures informs contemporary diplomatic strategies.

10. Conclusion: Navigating the Complexities:

In conclusion, the section underscores the complexities inherent in protocols on intervention and interference diplomacy. It emphasizes the ongoing challenge of developing ethical and effective frameworks that allow the international community to address crises while respecting the principles of state sovereignty and non-interference. As global dynamics evolve, diplomatic protocols must adapt to ensure a nuanced and principled approach to intervention in the pursuit of global peace and stability.

The chapter scrutinizes the protocols governing intervention and the nuances of interference diplomacy. It delves into the criteria, procedures, and challenges associated with diplomatic interventions, exploring the fine line between constructive engagement and unwarranted interference in the internal affairs of sovereign states.

11.4 Global Limitations of Democracy:

Global Limitations of Democracy

This section examines the broader global context in which democracies operate, exploring the challenges and limitations that impact the effectiveness and universality of democratic governance.

1. Geopolitical Power Dynamics:

Global limitations of democracy are often intertwined with geopolitical power dynamics. This subsection delves into how the influence of major powers can shape the democratic landscape. It considers instances where powerful nations may prioritize strategic interests over democratic values, impacting the ability of nations to fully embrace and sustain democratic governance.

2. Economic Inequalities and Democracy:

Economic inequalities on a global scale pose significant challenges to the realization of democratic ideals. This part of the section explores how disparities in wealth and resources can hinder the development and consolidation of democracies, leading to unequal political representation and decision-making processes.

3. Cultural Relativism and Democratic Values:

Cultural differences and relativism can become barriers to the universal acceptance of democratic values. The subsection examines how diverse cultural contexts may influence the interpretation and implementation of democratic principles, with some societies grappling with the tension between local cultural norms and global democratic standards.

4. Influence of Non-State Actors:

Beyond nation-states, non-state actors, such as multinational corporations and international organizations, exert considerable influence on global affairs. This part explores how the interests and actions of these entities can impact democratic governance, sometimes leading to outcomes that prioritize economic goals over democratic ideals.

5. Technological Challenges and Information Warfare:

The rapid advancement of technology introduces new challenges to democracy globally. This subsection considers the impact of information warfare, cyber threats, and the manipulation of digital platforms on democratic processes. It examines how technological advancements can be both a tool for democratization and a source of vulnerabilities for democratic institutions.

6. Global Migration and Identity Politics:

Global migration trends and identity politics contribute to challenges faced by democracies. This part explores how demographic shifts, cultural diversification, and the rise of identity-based politics can strain the inclusivity and cohesion of democratic societies, leading to debates about national identity and social cohesion.

7. Global Governance and Democratic Deficits:

International institutions and mechanisms of global governance may exhibit democratic deficits. This section examines how decisions made at the global level may lack democratic legitimacy and accountability, raising questions about the representation of nations in global decision-making processes.

8. Climate Change and Environmental Challenges:

The global challenge of climate change poses significant implications for democracies. This subsection explores how environmental issues can strain democratic governance as nations grapple with the need for collective action, adaptation, and the trade-offs between environmental sustainability and economic growth.

9. Multilateralism and Cooperation:

Global limitations also arise in the context of multilateral cooperation. This part examines how the effectiveness of global democratic initiatives, such as efforts to address crises or promote human rights, can be hindered by the lack of consensus among nations and geopolitical rivalries.

10. Conclusion: Navigating Global Realities:

In conclusion, this section emphasizes the need to navigate the complex global realities that impact the functioning of democracies. It underscores the interconnectedness of nations in addressing common challenges and highlights the importance of international cooperation and dialogue to overcome the global limitations that can impede the full realization of democratic ideals. As democracies adapt to the evolving global landscape, acknowledging and addressing these limitations becomes crucial for fostering a more inclusive, just, and resilient world.

This section widens the lens to examine global limitations on the promotion and sustenance of democracy. It considers geopolitical power dynamics, economic interests, and the influence of major global players in shaping the democratic landscape, reflecting on how these factors impact the democratic aspirations of African nations.

11.5 The Regional Blocks Conspiracy and Interest:

Exploring the influence of regional blocks, this part of the chapter investigates potential conspiracies and conflicting interests within these organizations. It analyzes how regional dynamics, economic considerations, and geopolitical interests may shape the stance of regional blocks on issues related to democracy and governance.

11.6 African Union; The Toothless Bulldog:

African Union: The Toothless Bulldog

This section critically examines the African Union's (AU) role in promoting and safeguarding democratic principles on the continent, analyzing its strengths, weaknesses, and the challenges that have led to its characterization as a "toothless bulldog."

1. Formation and Objectives:

The African Union was established with the noble objectives of promoting unity, peace, and development across the African continent. This subsection provides a brief overview of the AU's formation, highlighting its foundational principles and aspirations for a united and prosperous Africa.

2. Peace and Security Mandate:

The AU was entrusted with a crucial peace and security mandate, aimed at preventing conflicts, resolving disputes, and maintaining stability within member states. This part explores the AU's efforts in fulfilling this mandate and the challenges it faces in effectively addressing conflicts and crises.

3. Democratic Governance and Human Rights:

Democracy and respect for human rights are core tenets of the AU's agenda. This subsection assesses the AU's role in promoting democratic governance, safeguarding human rights, and addressing issues related to electoral processes and governance challenges within member states.

4. Challenges to Intervention:

Despite its mandate, the AU has faced challenges in intervening decisively in internal conflicts. This part analyzes the factors contributing to the AU's limitations, including issues of sovereignty, financial constraints, and the complex nature of conflicts on the continent.

5. Lack of Enforcement Mechanisms:

One of the criticisms leveled against the AU is the perceived absence of effective enforcement mechanisms. This subsection examines the limitations in the AU's ability to enforce its decisions, whether in the context of conflict resolution or the promotion of democratic values.

6. Funding and Resource Constraints:

Financial and resource constraints have been cited as impediments to the AU's effectiveness. This part explores the challenges the organization faces in securing adequate funding and resources to implement its initiatives, impacting its ability to intervene and fulfill its mandate.

7. Coordination and Unity Challenges:

The AU comprises diverse nations with varied interests and political dynamics. This section delves into the challenges of achieving unity and coordination among member states, examining how internal divisions may hinder the AU's effectiveness in addressing continental issues.

8. The Perception of Inaction:

Public perception plays a crucial role in evaluating the AU's effectiveness. This subsection explores instances where the AU has been criticized for perceived inaction in the face of crises, contributing to the characterization of the organization as a "toothless bulldog."

9. Reforms and Institutional Strengthening:

Recognizing its limitations, the AU has embarked on reform initiatives to enhance its effectiveness. This part discusses the ongoing efforts to strengthen AU institutions, improve coordination, and address the structural challenges that have impeded its ability to act decisively.

10. Lessons for the Future:

Drawing lessons from the AU's experiences, this section reflects on the need for adaptive strategies, robust enforcement mechanisms, and stronger cooperation among member states to elevate the AU's role in promoting democracy, peace, and security on the continent.

11. Conclusion: The Path Forward:

In conclusion, the section emphasizes the imperative for the AU to overcome its limitations and evolve into a more proactive force for positive change in Africa. It underscores the need for sustained reforms, financial investment, and collaborative efforts among member states to transform the AU from a perceived "toothless bulldog" into a formidable advocate for democratic governance, peace, and development across the African continent.

The chapter critically examines the African Union's role in promoting democracy on the continent. It delves into the challenges that the AU faces in effectively intervening in member states' affairs, earning it the metaphorical description of a "toothless bulldog." The section explores institutional limitations and possible reforms needed to enhance the AU's impact.

11.7 ECOWAS and the Tale of Indifference:

This section critically examines the role of the Economic Community of West African States (ECOWAS) in addressing democratic challenges within the West African region, focusing on instances where the organization has been accused of displaying indifference to pressing issues.

1. Formation and Mandate:

An overview of ECOWAS's formation and mandate sets the stage for understanding the organization's objectives, emphasizing its commitment to fostering economic integration, stability, and democratic governance within West Africa.

2. Early Successes in Conflict Resolution:

ECOWAS initially gained acclaim for its successful interventions in regional conflicts, particularly in Liberia and Sierra Leone. This part acknowledges the organization's positive contributions to conflict resolution during its early years.

3. Democratic Governance as a Pillar:

Democratic governance is a core pillar of ECOWAS's mandate. This subsection explores how the organization has positioned itself as a champion of democracy, with mechanisms in place to monitor elections, address governance challenges, and promote adherence to democratic principles among member states.

4. Challenges to Intervention:

Despite its mandate, ECOWAS has faced challenges in effectively intervening in member states facing democratic deficits. This part analyzes the factors contributing to the organization's limitations, including issues of sovereignty, divergent national interests, and the reluctance of member states to intervene in each other's internal affairs.

5. The Tale of Indifference:

The section delves into specific instances where ECOWAS has been criticized for perceived indifference to pressing issues. This includes cases where the organization has been slow to respond to political crises, allegations of human rights abuses, or challenges to democratic governance within member states.

6. Economic Interests vs. Democratic Values:

Examining the delicate balance between economic interests and democratic values within ECOWAS, this part explores how the organization navigates situations where member states prioritize economic considerations over democratic principles, potentially leading to a perceived lack of decisive action.

7. The Influence of Regional Power Dynamics:

Regional power dynamics can significantly impact ECOWAS's ability to address democratic challenges. This subsection explores how influential member states may shape the organization's responses based on their geopolitical interests, potentially contributing to a narrative of indifference.

8. Civil Society Engagement and Public Perception:

The role of civil society and public perception is crucial in evaluating ECOWAS's effectiveness. This part discusses how civil society engagement and the perception of the organization by the public can influence its actions, and how indifference to grassroots concerns may erode trust in ECOWAS's ability to champion democratic values.

9. ECOWAS Summit Diplomacy:

Summit diplomacy is a key aspect of ECOWAS's decision-making process. This section examines the dynamics of ECOWAS summits, exploring how the organization formulates responses to democratic challenges and whether these responses align with the expectations of member states and the international community.

10. Reforms and Lessons Learned:

Acknowledging the need for continuous improvement, this part discusses ongoing reforms within ECOWAS. It reflects on lessons learned from instances of perceived indifference and highlights the importance of adapting strategies to enhance the organization's responsiveness to democratic challenges.

11. Conclusion: Charting a Responsive Path:

In conclusion, the section emphasizes the importance of

ECOWAS charting a responsive path in addressing democratic challenges. It calls for sustained efforts to overcome instances of perceived indifference, promote democratic values, and strengthen the organization's role as a proactive force for stability and governance within the West African region.

Focusing on ECOWAS, this part of the chapter explores the organization's response to democratic challenges in West Africa. It scrutinizes instances of indifference, diplomatic hesitancy, and the effectiveness of ECOWAS in addressing political crises within the sub-region.

11.8 Lessons Learned:

Drawing lessons from the complex interplay of regional blocks and diplomatic engagements, this section reflects on the successes and shortcomings of regional interventions in promoting democracy. It considers the importance of strategic collaboration, adherence to diplomatic protocols, and the need for greater regional unity to address democratic deficits effectively.

11.9 Conclusion:

In conclusion, the intricate relationship between regional blocks, diplomatic limitations, and the promotion of democracy in Africa is a multifaceted narrative. The chapter emphasizes the lessons learned from historical and contemporary examples, highlighting the need for diplomatic prudence, institutional reforms within regional bodies, and a collective commitment to upholding democratic values. As African nations navigate these complexities, understanding the dynamics of regional diplomacy is crucial for fostering a democratic landscape that respects sovereignty while addressing systemic challenges.

Chapter 11 delves into the dynamic evolution of democratic values, exploring how these foundational principles have transformed over time and continue to shape the fabric of societies around the world. As we navigate the historical currents and contemporary challenges, this chapter illuminates the enduring essence of democracy and its profound impact on the human experience.

Historical Roots of Democratic Ideals

1. Athenian Experiment and Direct Democracy

The origins of democratic ideals trace back to ancient Athens, where the concept of direct democracy emerged. Citizens actively participated in decision-making, emphasizing the ideals of political equality and civic engagement. This historical experiment laid the groundwork for democratic principles that resonate through the ages.

2. Enlightenment Era and Individual Rights

The Enlightenment era ushered in a profound shift in democratic thought. Thinkers like John Locke and Jean-Jacques Rousseau emphasized the inherent rights of individuals, inspiring the inclusion of concepts such as liberty, equality, and the pursuit of happiness in the foundations of democratic governance.

Expansion of Democratic Principles

1. Suffrage Movements and Universal Right to Vote

The expansion of democratic principles unfolded through suffrage movements. From the women's suffrage movement to civil rights struggles, the fight for the universal right to vote became a driving force in democratizing societies and advancing the inclusion of diverse voices in political processes.

2. Human Rights and Global Democratic Standards

The post-World War II era witnessed the formulation of global democratic standards through the Universal Declaration of Human Rights. The recognition of fundamental rights and freedoms on an international scale underscored the universality of democratic values as essential elements of human dignity.

Contemporary Challenges to Democratic Values

1. Erosion of Trust and Rise of Populism

In the contemporary landscape, challenges such as the erosion of trust in democratic institutions and the rise of populism pose threats to core democratic values. Understanding these challenges is crucial for devising strategies to fortify the resilience of democratic ideals in the face of evolving societal dynamics.

2. Technology, Information, and Democratic Governance

Advancements in technology have reshaped the dynamics of democratic governance. The rapid dissemination of information, the influence of social media, and the challenges posed by disinformation highlight the need to adapt democratic values to the digital age while preserving the integrity of information and discourse.

The Inclusive Tapestry of Democratic Values

1. Inclusivity Beyond Borders

The evolution of democratic values emphasizes inclusivity beyond national borders. Recognizing the interconnectedness of global challenges, nations strive to uphold democratic principles by fostering international cooperation, solidarity, and a commitment to shared values.

2. Intersectionality and Diversity

Contemporary democratic values embrace intersectionality, acknowledging the interconnected nature of social identities and experiences. The emphasis on diversity in political representation, policy-making, and societal inclusion becomes a central tenet in shaping a more equitable and responsive democracy.

Future Horizons: Democratic Values in Flux

1. Environmental Stewardship and Sustainable Democracy

The future of democratic values intertwines with environmental stewardship. As societies grapple with climate change and ecological challenges, the concept of sustainable democracy emerges, emphasizing the responsibility of democratic governance to safeguard the planet for current and future generations.

Environmental stewardship and sustainable democracy represent the intersection of responsible environmental practices and democratic governance. This involves fostering a political and societal framework that prioritizes sustainable development, environmental protection, and the well-being of both current and future generations. Here are key aspects of the relationship between environmental stewardship and sustainable democracy:

1. Informed Decision-Making: Sustainable democracy encourages informed decision-making on environmental policies. This includes involving citizens in the decision-making process, providing them with accurate information about environmental issues, and considering their opinions and preferences.

2. Public Participation: A sustainable democracy emphasizes public participation in environmental decision-making. This

can involve engaging citizens in discussions about environmental policies, seeking their input on sustainable initiatives, and allowing them to actively contribute to environmental governance.

3. Environmental Justice: Sustainable democracy promotes environmental justice by ensuring that all individuals, regardless of socioeconomic status or background, have equal access to a healthy environment. This includes addressing environmental inequalities and avoiding the disproportionate burden of environmental issues on vulnerable communities.

4. Policy Consistency: In a sustainable democracy, environmental policies are consistent with long-term ecological sustainability. This involves developing policies that balance economic development with environmental conservation, considering the impact on ecosystems, biodiversity, and natural resources.

5. Environmental Laws and Regulations: A sustainable democracy enforces and continually improves environmental laws and regulations. This includes establishing legal frameworks that deter environmental degradation, holding polluters accountable, and adapting regulations to address emerging environmental challenges.

6. Interconnectedness of Issues: Recognizing the interconnectedness of environmental issues with other societal challenges is crucial in sustainable democracy. This involves understanding the links between environmental sustainability, economic development, social equity, and public health.

7. Green Technologies: Sustainable democracies encourage the development and adoption of green technologies. This includes supporting research and innovation in renewable energy, sustainable agriculture, waste reduction, and other environmentally friendly practices.

8. Global Cooperation: Addressing global environmental challenges requires international cooperation. Sustainable democracies actively participate in global efforts to combat climate change, protect biodiversity, and promote sustainable development on a global scale.

9. Accountability and Transparency: A sustainable democracy values accountability and transparency in environmental governance. This involves holding institutions and individuals accountable for their environmental responsibilities, disclosing relevant information, and ensuring transparency in decision-making processes.

10. Education and Awareness: Sustainable democracies prioritize environmental education and awareness. This includes educating citizens about the importance of environmental stewardship, climate change, and sustainable living practices to build an environmentally conscious society.

11. Long-Term Planning: Sustainable democracies engage in long-term planning for environmental sustainability. This involves setting clear goals, developing strategies for sustainable resource management, and considering the impact of policies on future generations.

By integrating environmental stewardship into democratic governance, societies can work towards a harmonious balance between human activities and the preservation of the planet's ecosystems, fostering a more sustainable and resilient future.

2. Technological Ethical Standards

As technology continues to advance, the ethical standards governing its use become pivotal for the future of democratic values. Striking a balance between technological innovation and preserving democratic ideals requires ongoing dialogue, adaptation, and the formulation of ethical frameworks.

Conclusion: Nurturing the Essence of Democracy

Nurturing the essence of democracy involves fostering the foundational principles, values, and practices that define democratic governance. Here are key elements in nurturing the essence of democracy:

1. Respect for Human Rights: Democracy thrives on the respect and protection of human rights. Nurturing democracy involves upholding individual freedoms, promoting equality, and safeguarding the rights of all citizens, irrespective of their background or beliefs.

2. Rule of Law: The rule of law is a cornerstone of democracy. Nurturing the essence of democracy requires a commitment to a legal framework that is just, transparent, and consistently applied. This ensures that no one is above the law and that legal processes are fair and impartial.

3. Political Pluralism: Democracy embraces diversity of opinions and ideas. Nurturing democracy involves creating an inclusive political environment where multiple parties and viewpoints can coexist, compete, and contribute to the democratic discourse.

4. Citizen Participation: Democracy is strengthened when citizens actively participate in the decision-making process. Nurturing democracy includes promoting civic engagement, providing opportunities for public participation, and ensuring that the voices of citizens are heard in policymaking.

5. Free and Fair Elections: Elections are a fundamental aspect of democracy. Nurturing the essence of democracy requires conducting free and fair elections, where citizens can choose their representatives without coercion or manipulation.

6. Independent Judiciary: An independent judiciary is crucial for upholding the rule of law and ensuring justice. Nurturing democracy involves safeguarding the independence of the judiciary, protecting it from undue influence, and respecting judicial decisions.

7. Accountability and Transparency: Democratic governance demands accountability and transparency. Nurturing democracy involves holding public officials accountable for their actions, ensuring transparency in government operations, and fostering a culture of openness.

8. Civil Society Engagement: A vibrant civil society plays a vital role in democracy. Nurturing democracy includes supporting the activities of civil society organizations, non-governmental organizations (NGOs), and grassroots movements that contribute to democratic governance.

9. Educating Citizens: An informed citizenry is essential for a healthy democracy. Nurturing democracy involves investing in civic education to empower citizens with the knowledge and skills needed to actively participate in democratic processes.

10. Conflict Resolution: Democracy requires mechanisms for peaceful conflict resolution. Nurturing the essence of democracy involves promoting dialogue, mediation, and reconciliation to address political differences and prevent the escalation of conflicts.

11. Protection of Minorities: A thriving democracy protects the rights of minority groups. Nurturing democracy includes creating a societal framework that safeguards the interests and rights of minorities, ensuring they are not marginalized or discriminated against.

12. Adaptability and Innovation: Societies evolve, and democracy must adapt to changing circumstances. Nurturing democracy involves fostering an environment where democratic institutions can innovate and adapt to address emerging challenges and societal needs.

13. Ethical Leadership: Leadership plays a crucial role in shaping the essence of democracy. Nurturing democracy

requires ethical leadership committed to the principles of democracy, accountability, and public service.

14. Public Trust: Trust is the foundation of a functioning democracy. Nurturing democracy involves building and maintaining public trust in democratic institutions through responsive governance, ethical conduct, and effective communication.

By embracing and reinforcing these elements, societies can actively contribute to the nurturing of the essence of democracy, ensuring that democratic principles endure and continue to serve as a foundation for just and inclusive governance.

As we reflect on the evolution of democratic values, it becomes clear that democracy is not a static concept but a living, breathing force that adapts to the challenges and aspirations of each era. Nurturing the essence of democracy involves a collective commitment to the principles of freedom, equality, and justice—a commitment that transcends time and guides humanity toward a future shaped by the enduring spirit of democratic ideals.

CHAPTER 12

THE IMPERATIVE OF CIVIC ENGAGEMENT

"Democracy cannot succeed unless those who express their

choice are prepared to choose wisely. The real safeguard of democracy, therefore, is education." – Franklin D. Roosevelt

Chapter 12 explores the imperative of civic engagement as a cornerstone of vibrant and resilient democracies. It delves into the role of informed and active citizenry in shaping the trajectory of democratic governance. From the importance of civic education to the impact of grassroots initiatives, this chapter underscores the vital role individuals play in the continued evolution and sustenance of democratic values.

The imperative of civic engagement is the idea that citizens have a duty and a responsibility to participate in the affairs of their society and to contribute to the common good. Civic engagement can take many forms, such as voting, volunteering, protesting, organizing, or educating oneself and others about the issues that affect one's community and the world. Civic engagement can also be seen as a way of empowering oneself and others to have a voice and a stake in the decisions that shape one's life and society.

Civic engagement is important for several reasons. First, it can enhance the quality and legitimacy of democracy by ensuring that the government is responsive and accountable to the people, and that the people are informed and involved in the political process. Second, it can foster social cohesion and trust by building relationships and networks among diverse groups of people who share common interests and values. Third, it can promote personal and collective well-being by providing opportunities for learning, growth, self-expression, and fulfillment. Fourth, it can address the challenges and problems that face one's community and the world by mobilizing resources, skills, and ideas to create positive change.

However, civic engagement is not without its challenges and obstacles. Some of the factors that may hinder civic engagement include lack of time, resources, information, or motivation; lack of access, representation, or influence; lack of civility, tolerance, or respect; lack of trust, confidence, or efficacy; and lack of recognition, support, or reward. These factors may vary depending on the context, culture, and history of each society and community.

Therefore, it is imperative that civic engagement is encouraged, supported, and facilitated by various actors and institutions, such as governments, civil society organizations, media, schools, families, and individuals. Some of the ways to do so include providing civic education and information; creating spaces and platforms for dialogue and deliberation; ensuring equal and inclusive participation and representation; fostering a culture of civic values and norms; and recognizing and rewarding civic contributions and achievements.

The Educational Foundation

1. Civic Education: Nurturing Informed Citizens

Civic education serves as the bedrock of civic engagement. Imagine a world where educational systems prioritize teaching students about democratic principles, governance structures, and the responsibilities of citizenship. Nurturing informed citizens from a young age becomes a crucial step in fostering a vibrant democratic society.

2. Lifelong Learning for Civic Literacy

The imperative of civic engagement extends throughout life. Lifelong learning programs, accessible to people of all ages, equip individuals with the knowledge and skills to critically evaluate information, participate in civic discourse, and actively contribute to the democratic process.

Grassroots Initiatives: The Power of Communities

1. Community Organizing for Change

Visualize communities coming together to address local issues and effect positive change. Grassroots initiatives, driven by engaged citizens, become catalysts for social, economic, and political transformation. The power of collective action at the community level ripples through the broader democratic landscape.

2. Civic Tech and Digital Platforms

In the digital era, envision the use of civic tech and online platforms to amplify grassroots initiatives. Online spaces become hubs for civic engagement, enabling citizens to connect, collaborate, and mobilize around shared goals. The democratization of information and activism transcends geographical boundaries.

Inclusive Participation: Diverse Voices, Diverse Perspectives

1. Representation and Inclusivity

Democracy thrives when diverse voices are heard and represented. Picture a political landscape where inclusivity is not only a goal but a reality. Initiatives promoting diverse representation in elected offices, decision-making bodies, and public discourse become integral to the health of democratic institutions.

2. Empowering Marginalized Communities

Envision concerted efforts to empower marginalized communities to participate fully in civic life. Programs addressing systemic barriers, promoting equity, and ensuring equal access to resources empower individuals who have historically been marginalized to become active contributors to the democratic process.

Accountability and Transparency

1. Citizen Oversight and Watchdog Organizations

Imagine a future where citizen oversight is a fundamental component of democratic governance. Citizen-led watchdog organizations, equipped with the tools to monitor governmental activities, hold officials accountable, and ensure transparency, become essential guardians of democratic values.

2. Open Government Initiatives

Envisage governments embracing open government initiatives. Transparency, accessibility of information, and citizen involvement in decision-making processes become standard practices. Open government fosters trust, encourages citizen participation, and reinforces the principles of democratic accountability.

Global Solidarity in Civic Engagement

1. Transnational Activism and Collaboration

Picture a world where citizens engage in transnational activism to address global challenges. The interconnectedness of global issues, from climate change to human rights, prompts individuals and communities to collaborate across borders, leveraging collective strength in the pursuit of common goals.

2. International Platforms for Civic Exchange

Envision international platforms dedicated to civic exchange and collaboration. These platforms facilitate the sharing of experiences, best practices, and strategies for civic engagement. The global community becomes a dynamic space for learning, dialogue, and mutual support in the journey toward democratic resilience.

Conclusion: A Call to Active Citizenship

As we conclude this exploration of the imperative of civic engagement, the call to active citizenship resonates. The future of democracy depends on the commitment of individuals to stay informed, participate in civic life, and contribute to the betterment of their communities. In the chapters to come, we will further explore the symbiotic relationship between civic engagement and the overall health of democratic societies, acknowledging that the strength of democracy lies in the hands of its engaged citizens.

CHAPTER 13

ADAPTIVE GOVERNANCE IN THE 21ST CENTURY

"In times of profound change, the learners inherit the earth, while the learned find themselves beautifully equipped to deal with a world that no longer exists." – Eric Hoffer

Chapter 13 delves into the necessity of adaptive governance in the 21st century, emphasizing the crucial role of flexible and responsive systems in addressing the evolving challenges faced by democracies. From the impact of technological advancements to the need for anticipatory policies, this chapter explores how governance structures can adapt to the dynamic landscape of the modern era.

The necessity of adaptive governance in the 21st century underscores the critical importance of flexible and responsive systems in effectively addressing the evolving challenges faced by democracies. Adaptive governance refers to the ability of governing structures and processes to adjust, learn, and innovate in response to changing circumstances, ensuring they remain effective and relevant. Here are key points emphasizing the crucial role of adaptive governance in the contemporary era:

1. Complex Challenges: The 21st century presents democracies with unprecedented and complex challenges, ranging from global pandemics and climate change to technological disruptions and geopolitical shifts. Adaptive governance acknowledges the dynamic nature of these challenges and the need for nimble responses.

2. Rapid Change: Societal, economic, and technological changes occur at an unprecedented pace. Adaptive governance recognizes that static and rigid systems are ill-equipped to navigate this rapid change and emphasizes the importance of continuous adaptation to new realities.

3. Resilience: Adaptive governance contributes to the resilience of democratic systems. It allows governments to absorb shocks, recover from crises, and proactively address emerging issues. Resilient systems are better positioned to maintain stability and public trust during turbulent times.

4. Innovation and Experimentation: An adaptive governance approach encourages innovation and experimentation. It provides the space for trying new policy solutions, learning from both successes and failures, and refining strategies based on real-time feedback and evidence.

5. Public Participation: Adaptive governance involves meaningful public participation. Engaging citizens in decision-making processes fosters a sense of ownership, ensures diverse perspectives are considered, and enhances the legitimacy of government actions.

6. Data-Driven Decision Making: The use of data and technology is integral to adaptive governance. Data-driven decision-making enables governments to assess the impact of policies, identify emerging trends, and make informed adjustments to better serve the needs of the population.

7. Collaboration and Networking: Adaptive governance emphasizes collaboration and networking. Governments work in partnership with various stakeholders, including non-governmental organizations, businesses, and international entities, to leverage collective intelligence and resources.

8. Agility in Policy Formation: Traditional, bureaucratic approaches to policy formulation may become obsolete in the face of rapid change. Adaptive governance prioritizes agility, allowing for swift responses to emerging issues and the timely implementation of effective policies.

9. Learning Organizations: Governments that embrace adaptive governance view themselves as learning organizations. They actively seek feedback, monitor outcomes, and use evaluation mechanisms to continuously improve their performance and responsiveness.

10. Long-Term Planning with Flexibility: While adaptive governance is responsive to short-term challenges, it also involves long-term planning with built-in flexibility. Anticipating future trends and planning for resilience ensures that democracies can adapt to evolving circumstances.

11. Climate and Environmental Adaptation: The environmental challenges of the 21st century, such as climate change, demand adaptive governance. Governments must be capable of adjusting policies and strategies to address the evolving impacts of environmental shifts on societies.

12. Crisis Preparedness: Adaptive governance is crucial for

crisis preparedness. Whether facing health crises, economic downturns, or security threats, the ability to adapt quickly and efficiently is essential for minimizing negative impacts.

13. Responsive Institutions: Adaptive governance requires institutions that are responsive to the diverse needs and aspirations of the population. Institutions must be designed to facilitate collaboration, inclusivity, and the effective delivery of public services.

14. Global Interconnectedness: The interconnectedness of global challenges necessitates adaptive governance at both national and international levels. Collaborative responses to issues like migration, cybersecurity, and public health underscore the importance of flexible governance structures.

The Pace of Change

1. Technological Acceleration

In the 21st century, technological advancements occur at an unprecedented pace. Imagine a world where governments embrace the challenges and opportunities presented by rapid technological acceleration. Adaptive governance becomes essential to harness the benefits of innovation while mitigating potential risks to privacy, security, and social cohesion.

2. Global Interconnectedness

Picture a global landscape where nations are intricately connected. Challenges such as climate change, pandemics, and economic shifts transcend borders. Adaptive governance involves collaborative approaches that recognize the interconnectedness of global issues and seek coordinated solutions.

Anticipatory Governance

1. Forecasting Future Challenges

Envision a governance system that goes beyond reacting to immediate issues and actively anticipates future challenges. The capacity to identify emerging trends, risks, and opportunities allows governments to proactively shape policies, ensuring they are well-prepared for the complexities of the evolving world.

2. Scenario Planning and Resilience

Adaptive governance incorporates scenario planning as a tool to navigate uncertainties. Governments engage in resilience-building strategies, considering various potential futures and preparing for a range of outcomes. This forward-looking approach enhances the ability to respond effectively to unexpected events.

Citizen-Centric Governance

1. Participatory Decision-Making

Imagine a democratic system where citizens actively contribute to decision-making processes. Adaptive governance prioritizes participatory approaches, leveraging technology to engage the public in policy discussions, fostering a sense of ownership and ensuring that policies align with the diverse needs of the population.

2. Feedback Loops and Iterative Processes

Envisage governance systems that embrace feedback loops and iterative processes. Continuous communication between citizens and policymakers allows for real-time adjustments, ensuring that policies remain relevant and responsive to the changing needs and preferences of the population.

Dynamic Policy Implementation

1. Flexibility in Policy Implementation

In an era of rapid change, policies must be flexible and adaptable. Governments that recognize the need for continuous evaluation and adjustment of policies based on real-world outcomes demonstrate adaptive governance. Flexibility in implementation allows for course corrections when needed.

2. Collaborative Networks and Public-Private Partnerships

Picture collaborative networks where governments work closely with the private sector, civil society, and academia. Adaptive governance leverages public-private partnerships and interdisciplinary collaborations to access diverse expertise, resources, and innovative solutions to complex challenges.

Digital Transformation and E-Governance

1. Digitally Empowered Governments

Envision governments fully leveraging digital transformation. Adaptive governance embraces e-governance, where digital platforms streamline administrative processes, enhance service delivery, and provide open channels for communication between citizens and authorities.

2. Cybersecurity and Data Privacy Safeguards

In the digital age, governments prioritize cybersecurity and robust data privacy safeguards. Adaptive governance ensures that technological advancements do not compromise the security and privacy of citizens, instilling trust in digital governance systems.

Conclusion: The Evolutionary Imperative

In conclusion, the necessity of adaptive governance in the 21st century is rooted in the acknowledgment that democracies must evolve and innovate to effectively address the complex and dynamic challenges of the contemporary era. By fostering flexibility, responsiveness, and continuous learning, adaptive governance ensures that democratic systems remain resilient and capable of meeting the evolving needs of societies.

As we conclude this exploration of adaptive governance in the 21st century, the evolutionary imperative becomes clear. Democracies that embrace adaptability, anticipatory strategies, and citizen-centric approaches are better equipped to navigate the complexities of our dynamic world. In the upcoming chapters, we will delve deeper into case studies and practical examples, illustrating how adaptive governance principles can be implemented to fortify democratic institutions and ensure their resilience in the face of ongoing changes.

CHAPTER 14

THE EVOLUTION OF DEMOCRATIC GOVERNANCE: NAVIGATING CHALLENGES AND SHAPING TOMORROW

""The preservation of democracy requires wisdom, diligence, and, above all, a committed citizenry." – Unknown

Democracy is widely regarded as the best form of governance that respects the dignity, freedom, and rights of all human beings. However, democracy is not a static or fixed concept, but rather a dynamic and evolving one, that constantly faces new challenges and opportunities in a complex and changing world. How can we ensure that democracy remains relevant, effective, and legitimate in the 21st century?

How can we adapt and improve the institutions and processes of democratic governance to meet the needs and aspirations of all people? How can we navigate the uncertainties and risks that threaten the stability and sustainability of democracy?

How can we shape the democracy of tomorrow, that is, a democracy that is more responsive, accountable, inclusive, collaborative, and resilient? These are some of the questions that this Chapter aims to explore, by analyzing the current and future trends and issues of democratic governance, and by proposing some ways to overcome the challenges and to enhance the quality and effectiveness of democracy.

In the grand narrative of human history, democracy emerged not as a static achievement but as a dynamic experiment, subject to the ebb and flow of societal currents. Chapter 14 of this exploration delves into the intricate evolution of democratic governance, acknowledging the challenges faced and the transformative potential embedded in each obstacle.

The Divergence Within

As the concept of democracy took root, the divergence within its core became a crucible for testing the resilience of its principles. The grand promise of equal representation collided with the human penchant for power, leading to instances where leaders, entrusted with the democratic mandate, veered towards authoritarian tendencies. This challenge tested the very essence of democracy, prompting reflection on the delicate balance between elected authority and the safeguarding of democratic ideals.

The Tapestry of Influence

Interwoven with the narrative of democracy is the intricate thread of money and influence. The promise of an equal voice for all citizens faced the relentless pull of financial interests, threatening to distort the democratic melody. The challenge lay not only in recognizing this encroachment but in formulating mechanisms to preserve the sanctity of the democratic process, ensuring that the chorus of the people prevailed over the discord of vested interests.

Inclusivity: The Unfinished Tapestry

Democracy's commitment to inclusivity encountered hurdles along its journey. The vision of a system where every citizen, irrespective of background or circumstance, contributes to the collective destiny faced the stark reality of systemic inequalities. The challenge became not only to acknowledge these disparities but to actively dismantle the barriers hindering the full participation of marginalized voices.

Lessons from the Crucible

While the challenges faced by democracy have been profound, they have also served as catalysts for transformation. The pages of history reveal not only the tales of divergence but also narratives of resilience, reform, and redemption.

1. Strengthening Democratic Institutions:

The response to divergence necessitated fortifying

democratic institutions. Checks and balances were reinforced, and the call for transparency became a driving force. Strengthening the pillars of democracy became an ongoing endeavor, ensuring that the lessons learned from challenges translated into enduring institutional resilience.

2. Civic Responsibility and Engagement:

The crucible of challenges underscored the indispensable role of an active citizenry. Democracy, it became evident, is not a spectator sport but a participatory venture. The commitment to preserving democratic values required citizens to engage, question, and hold leaders accountable, fostering a culture of civic responsibility.

3. Embracing Reform:

The evolution of democracy unfolded as a narrative of constant reform. Acknowledging the imperfections and actively pursuing reformative measures became integral to the democratic journey. From campaign finance reforms to initiatives promoting inclusivity, each reform contributed to shaping a more robust and responsive democratic system.

Charting the Path Forward

As we reflect on the challenges encountered in the evolution of democratic governance, it becomes evident that the story of democracy is one of perpetual growth. The grand tapestry of democracy, woven with the threads of divergence and resilience, continues to evolve.

In the chapters to come, we will explore the contemporary

landscape of democratic governance, delving into innovative solutions, successful case studies, and the ongoing efforts to further refine and fortify the democratic experiment. The journey of democracy is not a static tale; it is an ever-unfolding narrative shaped by the collective commitment of citizens to uphold the principles that lie at the heart of this remarkable human endeavor.

CHAPTER 15

DEMOCRATIC RENAISSANCE: INNOVATIONS AND ASPIRATIONS FOR TOMORROW

"The test of our progress is not whether we add more to the abundance of those who have much; it is whether we provide enough for those who have too little." – Franklin D. Roosevelt

Chapter 15 marks a pivotal juncture in our exploration—a reflection on the present landscape of democratic governance, innovations that have reshaped its contours, and the aspirations that guide us toward an inclusive and equitable future.

The Digital Frontier: Democratizing Information

In the 21st century, technology has emerged as a transformative force in democratic governance. Imagine a world where digital platforms serve as conduits for citizen engagement, enabling direct participation in decision-making processes. From online town halls to interactive policy platforms, the digital frontier has the potential to bridge the gap between citizens and policymakers, fostering a more inclusive democratic experience.

Blockchain and Electoral Integrity:

The advent of blockchain technology holds promise for enhancing electoral integrity. Picture a future where secure, transparent, and tamper-proof blockchain systems underpin electoral processes, ensuring the sanctity of every vote. The utilization of blockchain not only bolsters confidence in electoral outcomes but also sets new standards for global electoral best practices.

Global Collaborations: Strengthening Democratic Solidarity

In an era of interconnected challenges, envision a network of nations collaborating to fortify democratic values. Diplomatic alliances and international partnerships become not just symbolic gestures but active mechanisms for sharing knowledge, resources, and strategies. The global community unites in the pursuit of common goals—protecting democracy from external threats and ensuring its vibrancy in the face of shared challenges.

United Nations Sustainable Development Goals (SDGs):

The United Nations takes center stage in promoting democratic principles globally through initiatives like the Sustainable Development Goals (SDGs). The SDGs recognize the integral role of democratic governance in achieving sustainable development. The goals underscore the importance of inclusivity, justice, and accountable institutions as cornerstones of a thriving society.

Inclusive Governance: Elevating Marginalized Voices

Envisage a democracy where every citizen, regardless of background or circumstance, is not only heard but actively shapes the trajectory of governance. Inclusive governance initiatives prioritize marginalized voices, dismantling systemic barriers and ensuring that policies address the diverse needs of the population. Intersectionality becomes a guiding principle in policy formulation and representation.

Participatory Budgeting:

Participatory budgeting emerges as a powerful tool in fostering inclusive governance. Communities engage in direct decision-making regarding the allocation of public funds, ensuring that the distribution of resources reflects the priorities and aspirations of the entire citizenry.

Environmental Democracy: Sustaining the Planet

The democratic ethos extends to the stewardship of the environment. Envision a future where environmental concerns are at the forefront of democratic governance. Governments and citizens collaborate to address climate change, biodiversity loss, and ecological challenges, recognizing that the health of the planet is intricately linked to the well-being of democratic societies.

Green Initiatives and Policy Integration:

Green initiatives permeate democratic governance, influencing policies across sectors. The integration of environmental considerations into decision-making processes reflects a commitment to long-term sustainability and aligns with the aspirations of citizens who prioritize the preservation of the planet.

Adaptive Governance: Navigating Uncertainties

As challenges evolve, so must governance structures. Adaptive governance becomes not only a response to change but a proactive strategy. Governments anticipate future challenges, engage in scenario planning, and embrace continuous reform to ensure that democratic institutions remain agile and responsive to the needs of a dynamic society.

Crisis Response and Resilience:

Adaptive governance is exemplified in crisis response mechanisms. From pandemics to economic shocks, governments with resilient and adaptive structures effectively navigate uncertainties. The ability to learn, adjust, and innovate in the face of crises becomes a hallmark of successful democratic governance.

Citizen Empowerment: Beyond Voting Booths

Imagine a democracy where citizen empowerment extends beyond the act of voting. Lifelong civic education, digital literacy programs, and opportunities for civic engagement become integral components of a society where every individual is equipped to actively participate in shaping the collective future.

Digital Civic Spaces:

Virtual civic spaces emerge as vibrant arenas for dialogue and collaboration. Online platforms foster meaningful discussions, bridge divides, and enable citizens to contribute to the democratic discourse from the comfort of their digital spaces.

Conclusion: Charting the Democratic Horizon

As we reflect on the innovations and aspirations outlined in this chapter, it becomes evident that democracy, far from being a static concept, is a living, evolving system. The tapestry of democratic governance weaves together the threads of technological advancements, global collaborations, inclusive practices, environmental stewardship, and adaptive strategies.

In the chapters ahead, we will delve into case studies, explore practical examples, and continue our journey through the ever-changing landscape of democracy. The democratic horizon beckons, inviting us to actively contribute to the ongoing narrative of collective empowerment, equality, and justice for all.

CHAPTER 16

DEMOCRATIC RESILIENCE: NAVIGATING CHALLENGES AND THRIVING AMIDST UNCERTAINTIES

"Democracy is not a machine that would go of itself. It needs continual adjustment, frequent oiling, and in the first place, careful cleaning out." – John Jay Chapman

Chapter 16 embarks on an exploration of democratic resilience, delving into the mechanisms, values, and adaptations that enable democratic systems to withstand challenges and continue evolving in the face of uncertainties.

The Resilient Core of Democracy

Democracy, akin to a living organism, possesses an inherent resilience embedded in its core principles. Envision a resilient democratic system where the fundamental values of freedom, equality, and justice serve as an unwavering foundation. Despite external pressures and internal challenges, the essence of democracy endures, adapting and evolving to address the evolving needs of society.

Rule of Law and Democratic Stability:

The rule of law emerges as a bedrock of democratic resilience. A society governed by just laws, applied impartially, provides stability and confidence in the democratic process. The resilience of democracy is reflected in the adherence to legal frameworks that safeguard individual rights and ensure accountability.

Adapting to Technological Transformations

As technology continues to reshape the world, imagine a democracy that not only embraces innovation but harnesses its power for the common good. Technological advancements, rather than posing threats, become tools for enhancing democratic processes, ensuring transparency, and fostering citizen engagement.

Cybersecurity and Data Privacy Protections:

The resilience of democracy in the digital age relies on robust cybersecurity measures and stringent data privacy protections. Governments prioritize securing electoral processes and sensitive information, safeguarding the trust citizens place in digital governance systems.

Crisis Response and Adaptive Governance

In the face of crises, resilient democracies exhibit a capacity to respond swiftly and effectively. Picture a scenario where adaptive governance mechanisms come to the forefront during unforeseen challenges, providing a framework for coordinated responses and proactive solutions.

Pandemic Response and Healthcare Access:

The COVID-19 pandemic serves as a litmus test for democratic resilience. Nations with adaptable healthcare systems, transparent communication, and collaborative decision-making demonstrate the strength of democratic institutions in times of crisis. The crisis underscores the importance of accessible and equitable healthcare as a pillar of resilient democracies.

Inclusive Policies and Social Cohesion

The resilience of democracy is mirrored in its ability to foster social cohesion through inclusive policies. Visualize a society where policies actively address systemic inequalities, promoting inclusivity and ensuring that the benefits of democracy reach every corner of the population.

Equitable Resource Allocation and Social Welfare Programs:

Resilient democracies prioritize equitable resource

allocation, directing resources towards sectors that need them the most. Social welfare programs become instruments for addressing disparities, fostering social cohesion, and reinforcing the idea that democracy is a force for the collective well-being.

Citizen Education and Civic Engagement

The resilience of democracy is intricately tied to an informed and engaged citizenry. Envision a society where civic education is not just a part of formal schooling but a lifelong pursuit. Informed citizens actively participate in democratic processes, holding their leaders accountable and contributing to the vitality of democratic governance.

Media Literacy and Information Integrity:

In the age of information, resilient democracies prioritize media literacy. Citizens are equipped with the skills to critically evaluate information, discern disinformation, and actively engage in fact-based discourse. A resilient democracy relies on an informed public capable of making sound decisions.

International Collaboration and Solidarity

Democracy's resilience extends beyond national borders. Picture a world where nations collaborate, share best practices, and support one another in upholding democratic values. International alliances become a bulwark against threats to democracy, creating a global network committed to the preservation of democratic principles.

Democratic Diplomacy and Global Governance:

Resilient democracies engage in diplomatic efforts to promote democratic values globally. They contribute to international forums, support democratic movements, and actively participate in shaping global governance structures that prioritize human rights, peace, and sustainable development.

Conclusion: The Ongoing Journey

As we conclude this exploration of democratic resilience, the journey continues. Resilient democracies acknowledge that challenges are not impediments but opportunities for growth and adaptation. In the chapters ahead, we will delve into case studies, examine real-world examples, and continue to unravel the intricate tapestry of democratic governance, showcasing its enduring capacity to navigate uncertainties and thrive in the ever-changing landscape of human societies.

CHAPTER 17

DEMOCRATIC ACCOUNTABILITY

The Sentinel of Trust and Transparency

"The only way to hold a government accountable is to make it accountable." – Joseph Wood Krutch

Chapter 17 delves into the paramount importance of democratic accountability, exploring how transparency, checks and balances, and civic engagement form the linchpin of a robust democratic system. In a world where trust in institutions is both the currency and cornerstone of democracy, accountability emerges as the sentinel guarding the democratic edifice.

The Foundations of Trust

Trust is the lifeblood of democracy. Envision a society where citizens trust their government to act in their best interests, where institutions are regarded as custodians of public welfare. The foundations of this trust are laid upon the principles of transparency, ethical governance, and a shared commitment to democratic values.

Democratic accountability is a foundational principle within democratic governance that ensures those in power, whether elected representatives or government officials, are answerable and responsible to the people. It establishes mechanisms through which citizens can hold their leaders accountable for their actions, decisions, and policies. Here are key aspects and considerations related to democratic accountability:

1. Elections: Regular, free, and fair elections are a cornerstone of democratic accountability. Citizens have the power to choose their representatives, and elections provide an opportunity for people to express approval or disapproval of the government's performance.

2. Transparency: Transparency is vital for accountability. Governments must provide accessible and accurate information about their actions, policies, and expenditures. Openness enables citizens to make informed judgments about the performance of their leaders.

3. Rule of Law: Democratic accountability is closely tied to the rule of law. Leaders, including those in the highest offices, are subject to the same laws as ordinary citizens. An independent judiciary ensures that legal standards are upheld and that those in power can be held accountable for any misconduct.

4. Citizen Participation: Active citizen participation is crucial for holding leaders accountable. This includes not only voting but also engaging in civic activities, expressing opinions, and participating in public discourse. Civil society plays a vital role in fostering citizen involvement.

5. Media Freedom: A free and independent media acts as a watchdog, bringing issues of public concern to light and scrutinizing the actions of those in power. Media freedom is essential for informing the public and facilitating accountability.

6. Oversight Institutions: Effective oversight institutions, such as ombudsman offices, audit institutions, and anti-corruption bodies, contribute to democratic accountability. These institutions monitor the government's activities and investigate allegations of malfeasance.

7. Civil Liberties: Protecting civil liberties, including freedom of speech and assembly, is fundamental for democratic accountability. Citizens must feel secure in expressing their opinions and participating in peaceful protests without fear of reprisal.

8. Responsive Governance: Leaders must be responsive to the needs and concerns of the people. Regular communication, town hall meetings, and mechanisms for public feedback contribute to a responsive and accountable government.

9. Decentralization: Devolving power to local levels through decentralization can enhance democratic accountability. Local governments that are closer to the people are often more responsive and accountable to local needs.

10. Political Culture: A democratic political culture that values accountability and ethical conduct is essential. This includes fostering a sense of responsibility among leaders and citizens alike.

11. Ethical Leadership: Ethical leadership is a key component of democratic accountability. Leaders who adhere to ethical standards and integrity contribute to public trust and confidence in the democratic process.

12. Recall Mechanisms: Some democratic systems include recall mechanisms, allowing citizens to petition for the removal of elected officials before the end of their term if they are dissatisfied with their performance.

13. International Accountability: In an interconnected world, international accountability also plays a role. Nations may be held accountable for human rights abuses or violations of international agreements through mechanisms such as international tribunals or diplomatic pressure.

14. Education and Awareness: A well-informed citizenry is better equipped to hold leaders accountable. Educational initiatives that promote civic literacy and political awareness contribute to a more engaged and accountable society.

Transparency as a Pillar of Trust:

Trust thrives in the light of transparency. Resilient democracies prioritize openness in decision-making processes, ensuring that citizens have access to information that informs and empowers them. Transparent governance becomes a bridge connecting the people and their representatives.

Checks and Balances: Safeguarding Against Abuse of Power

Democracy flourishes when power is not concentrated but diffused and balanced. Picture a system where checks and balances are not just theoretical concepts but active mechanisms that prevent the abuse of power. Independent judiciaries, vigilant media, and a robust legislative process serve as safeguards against overreach.

Judicial Independence:

The judiciary, vested with the responsibility of upholding the rule of law, plays a pivotal role in holding governments accountable. Judicial independence ensures that legal decisions are made impartially, free from undue influence, contributing to the trust citizens place in the justice system.

Civic Oversight: Empowering the Watchdogs

In a thriving democracy, citizens are not mere observers but active participants in the oversight process. Envision a scenario where civic watchdogs, empowered by information and protected by whistleblowing mechanisms, actively contribute to holding institutions accountable. Civil society organizations, investigative journalism, and citizen-led initiatives become vital components of the democratic checks and balances.

Whistleblower Protection:

The resilience of democratic accountability rests on the protection of whistleblowers. Whistleblowing mechanisms empower individuals to expose corruption, misconduct, and abuses of power without fear of reprisal. A society that values and protects whistleblowers fosters an environment of accountability.

Responsive Governance: Adapting to Citizen Feedback

A responsive government is one that not only listens but acts on the concerns and feedback of its citizens. Visualize a democracy where mechanisms for citizen input go beyond elections, encompassing ongoing channels for feedback on policies, services, and governance. The responsiveness of government becomes a testament to its accountability.

Citizen Feedback Loops:

In the digital age, technology facilitates real-time citizen feedback loops. Governments actively seek input through digital platforms, town hall meetings, and community forums. The iterative nature of these feedback mechanisms ensures that policies remain aligned with the evolving needs and expectations of the public.

Electoral Integrity: Safeguarding the Voice of the People

Elections are the cornerstone of democratic expression, and their integrity is non-negotiable. Picture an electoral system where every citizen's vote is not just a right but a sacred trust. Robust electoral processes, secure from interference, ensure that the voice of the people is accurately and fairly represented.

Election Security Measures:

Resilient democracies invest in comprehensive election security measures. From safeguarding voter registration databases to securing electronic voting systems, the integrity of the electoral process is upheld, preserving the cornerstone of democratic legitimacy.

Anti-Corruption Measures: Upholding Ethical Governance

Corruption erodes the very foundations of democratic trust. Envision a society where anti-corruption measures are not merely reactive but proactive, preventing corruption before it takes root. Transparent financial systems, independent anti-corruption bodies, and a culture of ethical governance become bulwarks against corruption.

Independent Anti-Corruption Agencies:

Independent agencies, empowered to investigate and prosecute corruption, exemplify a commitment to ethical governance. Their autonomy ensures that anti-corruption efforts are conducted without political interference, contributing to the trust citizens place in the integrity of their institutions.

Conclusion: The Covenant of Trust

As we conclude our exploration of democratic accountability, the essence becomes clear—it is a covenant of trust between the governed and their governors. Resilient democracies recognize that accountability is not a one-time commitment but an ongoing process, an ever-vigilant guardian that ensures the democratic promise endures.

Democratic accountability is not a one-size-fits-all concept; its effectiveness can vary based on cultural, historical, and institutional contexts. However, it remains a fundamental principle for the functioning of democratic systems, ensuring that power is exercised in the best interests of the people.

In the chapters ahead, we will delve into case studies, examine the real-world impact of accountability mechanisms, and continue our journey through the multifaceted landscape of democratic governance. The sentinel of accountability stands as a testament to the strength of democracy—a system that, when held accountable, thrives, adapts, and remains true to the ideals of freedom, equality, and justice for all.

CHAPTER 18

DEMOCRATIC PLURALISM: EMBRACING DIVERSITY FOR COLLECTIVE PROSPERITY

"Diversity is not about how we differ. Diversity is about embracing one another's uniqueness." – Ola Joseph

Chapter 18 embarks on a journey through the vital concept of democratic pluralism, celebrating the richness that diversity brings to the fabric of governance. In a resilient democracy, pluralism is not only acknowledged but actively embraced, fostering an inclusive environment where a myriad of voices, perspectives, and experiences converge for the collective prosperity of the society.

Democratic pluralism is a foundational concept in democratic theory that emphasizes the acceptance and encouragement of diverse perspectives, beliefs, and interests within a society. It recognizes that societies are inherently diverse, with individuals and groups holding different values, ideologies, and identities. Instead of seeking to impose a single, uniform worldview, democratic pluralism advocates for the inclusion and equal consideration of diverse voices in the decision-making processes of a democratic society.

Democratic pluralism is a political concept that refers to the recognition and affirmation of diversity within a political community. It allows for the peaceful coexistence of different interests, convictions, and lifestyles. Democratic pluralism is often seen as the most desirable form of democracy, because it respects the rights and freedoms of individuals and groups to express their views and participate in decision-making.

Some of the features of democratic pluralism are:

- Multiple centers of power: In a democratic pluralism, power is dispersed among a variety of economic and ideological pressure groups and is not monopolized by a single elite or group of elites. This ensures that no one group can dominate the political system and that different perspectives are represented and balanced.

- Electoral coalitions: In a democratic pluralism, individuals achieve positions of formal political authority by forming successful electoral coalitions. These coalitions are formed through a process of bargaining among political leaders and subleaders of the various organizations within the community. This encourages dialogue and compromise among different factions and interests.

- Institutional design: In a democratic pluralism, the design of political institutions reflects and accommodates the diversity of the society. For example, a pluralist democracy may adopt a federal system, a proportional representation system, a bicameral legislature, a constitutional court, or a bill of rights to protect the rights and interests of minorities and prevent the tyranny of the majority.

- Pluralization: In a democratic pluralism, the goal is not only to accept diversity, but also to promote it. Pluralization is the process of multiplying and diversifying the factions and groups within a society, as well as the values and principles they uphold. [3] This fosters a culture of tolerance and respect for difference, as well as a sense of civic engagement and participation.

Key principles and characteristics of democratic pluralism include:

1. Inclusivity: Democratic pluralism promotes the inclusion of all individuals and groups, irrespective of their backgrounds, identities, or beliefs, in the democratic process. It recognizes the inherent worth and dignity of each member of society.

2. Respect for Diversity: It acknowledges and values the diversity of opinions, cultures, religions, and lifestyles

present within a society. Rather than seeking conformity, democratic pluralism celebrates differences as a source of strength and richness.

3. Equal Participation: In a democratically pluralistic system, all citizens are afforded equal opportunities to participate in political processes. This includes the right to vote, express opinions, and engage in civic activities without discrimination.

4. Protection of Minority Rights: Democratic pluralism emphasizes the protection of minority rights. It ensures that minority groups are not marginalized or excluded, and their rights are safeguarded against the potential tyranny of the majority.

5. Freedom of Expression: An essential component of democratic pluralism is the freedom of expression. Individuals should be free to express their opinions, ideas, and beliefs without fear of repression, fostering an environment of open dialogue and debate.

6. Rule of Law: Democratic pluralism operates within the framework of the rule of law. Legal mechanisms are in place to protect the rights of individuals and ensure that decisions are made in accordance with established laws and procedures.

7. Tolerance: Tolerance is a core value of democratic pluralism. It encourages a society where people with

differing views or backgrounds can coexist peacefully, recognizing that diversity is an intrinsic aspect of human societies.

8. Compromise and Consensus: In situations of conflicting interests, democratic pluralism encourages the search for compromise and consensus. Decision-making processes involve negotiation and dialogue to find common ground that respects the concerns of various stakeholders.

9. Democratic Institutions: Robust democratic institutions, such as independent judiciaries, free media, and transparent electoral systems, are essential for the functioning of democratic pluralism. These institutions help ensure that power is distributed, and checks and balances are maintained.

10. Civic Education: Promoting civic education is crucial for fostering democratic pluralism. Citizens need to be informed about their rights, the political process, and the importance of respecting diverse perspectives to actively participate in a pluralistic democracy.

11. Accountability: Democratic pluralism necessitates accountability from those in power. Elected officials and institutions must be accountable to the people they serve, and mechanisms should be in place to address any abuses of power.

12. Social Cohesion: While recognizing and embracing diversity, democratic pluralism also seeks to build social cohesion. It emphasizes the shared values and goals that

unite individuals across their differences.

13. Adaptability: Democratic pluralism acknowledges that societies evolve, and it promotes adaptability to changing demographics, attitudes, and challenges. It seeks to ensure that democratic principles remain relevant and inclusive over time.

In summary, democratic pluralism stands as an alternative to authoritarian or homogenizing approaches to governance. By embracing and celebrating diversity, it aims to create a more inclusive, just, and vibrant democratic society where the collective prosperity is advanced through the participation and contributions of all its members.

The Mosaic of Diversity

Picture a democracy as a vibrant mosaic, where each individual represents a unique tile contributing to the overall tapestry of the nation. In a pluralistic democracy, diversity is not merely tolerated but celebrated as an essential and defining characteristic.

Some examples of democratic pluralism are:

- **New Zealand**: New Zealand is a parliamentary democracy that has a proportional representation system, which ensures that the seats in the legislature reflect the votes of the people. New Zealand also has a strong tradition of civil society and interest groups that advocate for various causes and issues, such as environmentalism, human rights, and indigenous rights. New Zealand is also known for its multiculturalism and diversity, as it recognizes the rights and interests of the Maori people, the Pacific Islanders, and other ethnic and religious minorities.

- **Switzerland:** Switzerland is a federal republic that has a direct democracy system, which allows the citizens to initiate and vote on referendums and popular initiatives on various matters of national and local importance. Switzerland also has a consociational democracy system, which ensures that the four major linguistic and cultural groups (German, French, Italian, and Romansh) share power and cooperate in the government. Switzerland also has a vibrant civil society and a pluralistic media that represent and promote the views and interests of different segments of the society.

- **India:** India is the world's largest democracy that has a parliamentary system with a multi-party system, which reflects the diversity and complexity of the Indian society. India also has a federal system that grants a degree of autonomy and self-government to the 28 states and 8 union territories. India also has a secular constitution that guarantees the freedom of religion and the protection of the rights and interests of various religious and ethnic minorities, such as the Muslims, Sikhs, Christians, Dalits, and Adivasis. India also has a vibrant civil society and a pluralistic media that engage in various forms of social and political activism and advocacy.

Cultural Diversity: A National Asset:

Resilient democracies recognize cultural diversity as a

national asset. Diverse traditions, languages, and customs contribute to the cultural richness of the nation. Policies that preserve and promote cultural diversity become integral to a society's identity.

Inclusive Representation: A Tapestry of Voices

In an inclusive democracy, representation mirrors the diverse composition of the population. Envision a scenario where elected bodies, decision-making bodies, and public offices reflect the full spectrum of society, ensuring that every community has a voice in the governance process.

Affirmative Action and Representation:

Affirmative action policies actively work to rectify historical imbalances and ensure equitable representation. Whether in political offices, corporate boardrooms, or public institutions, affirmative action becomes a catalyst for creating a more inclusive and representative democracy.

Gender Equality: Empowering Half the Sky

A resilient democracy prioritizes gender equality as a fundamental tenet. Visualize a society where gender-based discrimination is eradicated, and women are not just included but actively empowered to participate in all facets of public life.

Gender-Inclusive Policies:

Policies that promote gender inclusivity go beyond mere

rhetoric. Maternity and paternity leave, equal pay measures, and initiatives to break down gender stereotypes contribute to the creation of a society where every individual, regardless of gender, has equal opportunities.

Religious and Ethnic Pluralism: A Harmonious Coexistence

Imagine a democracy where religious and ethnic diversity is not a source of division but a testament to the richness of human experience. In a resilient society, policies are designed to foster understanding, tolerance, and harmonious coexistence among diverse religious and ethnic communities.

Interfaith Dialogue and Understanding:

Interfaith dialogue initiatives become catalysts for fostering understanding and collaboration among diverse religious communities. Education programs, community events, and dialogue forums contribute to a society where religious pluralism is celebrated.

Socioeconomic Inclusion: Bridging the Opportunity Gap

Resilient democracies actively work to bridge the gap between the privileged and the marginalized. Picture a society where socioeconomic status does not determine one's access to opportunities, and policies are designed to uplift the disadvantaged and ensure equal access to education, healthcare, and economic opportunities.

Poverty Alleviation Programs:

Policies focused on poverty alleviation become cornerstones

of a pluralistic democracy. Targeted programs that address systemic inequalities, provide social safety nets, and empower marginalized communities contribute to a more inclusive and egalitarian society.

Legal Protections and Anti-Discrimination Measures:

Robust legal frameworks ensuring protection against discrimination and hate crimes. Public policies actively work to create an inclusive environment that respects and celebrates diverse sexual orientations and gender identities.

Education for Pluralism: Nurturing Inclusive Mindsets

The resilience of democratic pluralism begins with education. Visualize a curriculum that not only imparts knowledge but fosters empathy, tolerance, and an appreciation for diversity. Educational institutions become incubators for nurturing inclusive mindsets from an early age.

Diversity and Inclusion Training:

In workplaces, government agencies, and civil society organizations, diversity and inclusion training become integral. These programs go beyond token gestures, fostering a culture where diversity is not just acknowledged but actively embraced as a source of strength.

Conclusion: The Symphony of Pluralism

As we conclude this exploration of democratic pluralism, the metaphorical symphony of diverse voices resonates. Resilient democracies recognize that true strength lies in unity amid diversity. In the chapters to come, we will delve into case studies, examine practical applications, and continue our journey through the kaleidoscopic landscape of democratic governance, celebrating the multitude of colors that contribute to the harmonious tapestry of a pluralistic society.

CHAPTER 19

DEMOCRATIC RENEWAL: ENGAGING THE NEXT GENERATION IN GOVERNANCE

"The future depends on what you do today." – *Mahatma Gandhi*

Chapter 19 unfolds the imperative of democratic renewal, emphasizing the pivotal role of the next generation in shaping the trajectory of governance. In a resilient democracy, the torch of responsibility is passed to the youth, instilling in them a sense of civic duty, active engagement, and a commitment to upholding the democratic values that underpin the society.

Democratic renewal refers to the process of revitalizing and strengthening democratic systems and institutions to ensure their continued relevance and effectiveness. One crucial aspect of democratic renewal is engaging the next generation in governance. In this context, the term "next generation" refers to young people who will be the future leaders and decision-makers in society.

Engaging the next generation in governance is essential for several reasons. First and foremost, young people have a stake in the future and should have a say in shaping it. They bring fresh perspectives, innovative ideas, and a deep understanding of the challenges and opportunities of their time. By involving them in governance, we can tap into their energy, enthusiasm, and creativity to address complex societal issues.

Furthermore, engaging young people in governance can help bridge the democratic deficit that often exists between generations. Many young people feel disconnected from traditional political processes and institutions, perceiving them as inaccessible, unresponsive, or unrepresentative. By actively involving them in decision-making, we can strengthen their trust in democratic systems and demonstrate that their voices matter.

There are several strategies and approaches to engage the next generation in governance. One of the most fundamental steps is to provide quality civic education in schools and universities. By teaching young people about democratic principles, institutions, and processes, we can equip them with the knowledge and skills necessary for active citizenship.

Beyond education, it's crucial to create platforms and mechanisms for meaningful youth participation in decision-making. This can include establishing youth advisory boards, organizing youth parliaments or summits, and integrating young people into decision-making bodies at different levels of government. These initiatives should not be symbolic gestures but should genuinely involve young people in shaping policies, influencing legislation, and designing programs that affect their lives.

Moreover, embracing technology and digital platforms can be instrumental in engaging the next generation. Young people are digital natives, and they often prefer to participate in civic and political processes through online platforms. Governments can leverage social media, online consultations, and participatory platforms to reach out to young people, gather their input, and involve them in decision-making.

Political parties and organizations also have a vital role to play in engaging the next generation. They should actively recruit and promote young leaders, create mentorship programs, and provide opportunities for young people to gain practical experience in governance. By nurturing young talent and providing them with meaningful roles, political entities can ensure a smooth transition of power and inject new perspectives into policy debates.

Lastly, it is crucial to foster a culture of inclusivity and respect for diverse voices. Engaging the next generation in governance should be inclusive of young people from all backgrounds, including those from marginalized communities. Efforts should be made to address barriers such as gender inequality, socioeconomic disparities, and discrimination that may hinder young people's participation.

Empowering Youth: The Catalyst for Change

Envision a democracy where the energy, creativity, and idealism of the youth are harnessed as catalysts for positive transformation. Resilient democracies actively empower and involve the younger generation, recognizing them not as passive recipients but as active architects of the nation's future.

Young people have the potential to drive positive transformations, challenge the status quo, and shape the future. By providing them with opportunities, resources, and support, we can unleash their creativity, passion, and leadership to address pressing issues and bring about meaningful change.

One of the key aspects of empowering youth is providing them with quality education. Education equips young people with knowledge, critical thinking skills, and a broader understanding of the world. It enables them to analyze societal problems, develop innovative solutions, and advocate for their ideas effectively. Accessible and inclusive education systems that prioritize quality learning for all can empower young people to become active participants in shaping their communities.

Beyond education, mentorship and guidance play crucial roles in empowering youth. Mentors can provide guidance, support, and encouragement to young individuals, helping them navigate challenges and develop their talents and skills. Mentors can share their experiences, provide valuable insights, and serve as role models for aspiring young change makers. Establishing mentorship programs and networks can create meaningful connections between experienced leaders and enthusiastic youth.

Moreover, creating platforms for youth participation is essential. Youth-led organizations, clubs, and initiatives provide spaces for young people to collaborate, express their opinions, and take collective action. These platforms enable young individuals to work together, amplify their voices, and address issues that directly affect them and their communities. Governments, civil society organizations, and community leaders should actively involve young people in decision-making processes, policy development, and implementation.

Empowering youth also means providing them with opportunities for meaningful engagement in social, economic, and political spheres. This can be achieved by promoting youth entrepreneurship and innovation, creating job opportunities, and supporting youth-led initiatives. Governments and businesses can establish funding mechanisms, mentorship programs, and incubators to nurture young entrepreneurs and innovators. By empowering young people economically, we enable them to contribute to society, create employment opportunities for others, and drive economic growth.

Furthermore, it is essential to recognize and address the unique challenges and barriers that young people face. These challenges include limited access to resources, discrimination, social exclusion, and marginalization. Empowering youth requires creating inclusive environments that value diversity, promote equality, and provide equal opportunities for all young individuals, regardless of their gender, ethnicity, socioeconomic background, or abilities.

Lastly, it is crucial to listen to the voices of young people and take their perspectives into account. Their experiences and insights can provide valuable contributions to policy development and decision-making processes. Engaging young people through surveys, consultations, and participatory mechanisms ensures that their opinions are heard and considered in shaping policies that impact their lives.

In conclusion, empowering youth is a catalyst for change. By investing in their education, providing mentorship, creating platforms for participation, offering economic opportunities, and addressing their unique challenges, we can unleash the potential of young people to drive positive transformations in society. Empowered youth bring fresh perspectives, innovative ideas, and a passion for creating a better world. By nurturing and supporting them, we can build inclusive and thriving communities for the future.

Civic Education and Engagement:

Civic education and engagement are essential components of a vibrant and healthy democracy. Civic education refers to the process of equipping individuals with the knowledge, skills, and values necessary to be active and responsible citizens. It provides an understanding of democratic principles, institutions, rights, and responsibilities, as well as the ability to engage in thoughtful and informed civic participation.

Civic education plays a crucial role in fostering informed and engaged citizens. It helps individuals understand the foundations of democracy, such as the rule of law, human rights, and the importance of civic participation. By learning about the political system, the electoral process, and the functions of government, individuals can make informed decisions and actively participate in shaping public policies.

In a democratic renewal, civic education goes beyond textbooks. It becomes a dynamic process that empowers young minds with the knowledge and skills necessary for active citizenship. Schools and communities collaborate to foster a culture of civic engagement from an early age.

Digital Democracy: Harnessing Technology for Civic Participation

Picture a society where technology is not just a tool but a gateway for youth participation in governance. Resilient democracies leverage digital platforms to provide accessible channels for young voices to be heard, fostering a sense of inclusion and enabling them to actively contribute to the democratic discourse.

Harnessing technology for civic participation has the potential to revolutionize the way people engage in democratic processes and contribute to public decision-making. Technology provides new avenues for citizens to connect, access information, voice their opinions, and collaborate on collective action. Here are some ways in which technology can be used to enhance civic participation:

1. Online Platforms for Information and Engagement: Technology allows for the creation of online platforms that provide easy access to information about government policies, legislative processes, and public initiatives. These platforms can enable citizens to stay informed, understand

complex issues, and express their opinions through online consultations, surveys, and feedback mechanisms. They can also facilitate online discussions and forums where citizens can exchange ideas and perspectives.

2. E-Participation and Digital Democracy: Technology can enable e-participation, where citizens can contribute to decision-making processes through digital means. Online platforms can be used to gather public input on policy issues, solicit feedback on proposed legislation, and involve citizens in the drafting of policies. This allows for a broader and more inclusive participation, as it removes geographical barriers and accommodates different schedules.

3. Crowdsourcing and Collaborative Problem-Solving: Technology enables crowdsourcing, which is the practice of soliciting ideas, solutions, and expertise from a large group of people. Governments and organizations can leverage online platforms to crowdsource innovative ideas, solutions to complex problems, and public input on various topics. This approach encourages citizen engagement, fosters collective intelligence, and promotes collaboration between government and citizens.

4. Open Data and Transparency: Technology can facilitate the availability and accessibility of government data through open data initiatives. Open data refers to the practice of making government information freely available for public use and analysis. By providing access to data on budgets, public services, and government performance, technology

enhances transparency and enables citizens to hold their governments accountable. It also allows for the development of data-driven tools and visualizations that help citizens understand and analyze public information.

5. Social Media and Digital Activism: Social media platforms have become powerful tools for civic participation and activism. They provide spaces for citizens to organize, mobilize, and advocate for social and political causes. Hashtags, online petitions, and viral campaigns are examples of how social media can amplify citizens' voices, raise awareness about issues, and catalyze collective action.

6. Civic Tech and Mobile Applications: Civic tech refers to the use of technology to enhance civic engagement and improve public services. Mobile applications can facilitate citizen reporting of problems, such as infrastructure issues or environmental concerns, and enable direct communication with government officials. They can also provide information on public services, voting locations, and civic events, making civic participation more accessible and convenient.

However, it's important to acknowledge that the digital divide and unequal access to technology can hinder inclusive civic participation. Efforts should be made to bridge the digital divide by ensuring equal access to technology and digital literacy programs. Additionally, privacy and security concerns must be addressed to protect citizens' data and ensure the integrity of online participation platforms.

In conclusion, technology offers tremendous opportunities to enhance civic participation by providing new avenues for information, engagement, collaboration, and activism. By leveraging technology effectively and addressing its limitations, governments, organizations, and citizens can harness its potential to create more inclusive, transparent, and participatory democratic processes.

Digital Platforms for Youth Participation:

Online forums, social media, and interactive platforms become spaces where the youth can voice their opinions, propose ideas, and engage in constructive dialogue. Digital democracy transcends geographical boundaries, ensuring that diverse youth perspectives shape the national narrative.

Youth Representation: A Seat at the Table

In a resilient democracy, the representation of the youth is not tokenistic but substantive. Envision a scenario where young leaders actively participate in decision-making bodies, ensuring that policies and initiatives address the unique challenges and aspirations of their demographic.

Youth Quotas and Leadership Programs:

Resilient democracies implement mechanisms such as youth quotas in political positions and leadership development programs to actively promote the inclusion of young voices in governance. These initiatives serve as incubators for the next generation of political leaders.

Mentorship and Inter-Generational Collaboration

The transition towards democratic renewal involves a symbiotic relationship between generations. Visualize a society where experienced leaders actively mentor and collaborate with the youth, providing guidance, sharing insights, and creating a bridge between the wisdom of experience and the innovation of youth.

Inter-Generational Dialogue Forums:

Regular forums, both formal and informal, become platforms for inter-generational dialogue. These spaces facilitate the exchange of ideas, perspectives, and knowledge, fostering a mutual understanding that strengthens the fabric of democratic governance.

Youth-Led Initiatives: From Activism to Governance

Imagine a democracy where youth-led initiatives not only advocate for change but actively participate in the governance process. Resilient democracies provide avenues for young activists to transition into roles where they can directly influence policies and contribute to the implementation of positive change.

Youth Policy Councils:

Establishing youth policy councils and advisory boards becomes a hallmark of democratic renewal. These councils serve as mechanisms for direct youth input into the decision-making process, ensuring that policies are reflective of the diverse needs and aspirations of the younger generation.

Global Youth Collaboration: Beyond Borders

In an interconnected world, envision a scenario where young people actively collaborate across borders, sharing ideas, perspectives, and solutions to common challenges. Resilient democracies actively promote international youth partnerships, recognizing that global issues require global collaboration.

Youth Exchanges and Diplomatic Programs:

Exchange programs, diplomatic initiatives, and collaborative projects become avenues for youth from different nations to interact, learn from one another, and collectively contribute to the advancement of democratic principles on a global scale.

Youth-Led Social Innovation: Tackling Contemporary Challenges

The challenges faced by society are ever-evolving, and in a democracy undergoing renewal, young minds become engines of innovation. Picture a scenario where youth-led initiatives address pressing issues such as climate change, social justice, and technological ethics, contributing fresh perspectives and solutions.

Social Entrepreneurship and Innovation Hubs:

Resilient democracies actively support youth-led social entrepreneurship and innovation hubs. These initiatives provide resources, mentorship, and platforms for young innovators to turn their ideas into impactful projects that address societal challenges.

Conclusion: Nurturing the Seeds of Democracy

In conclusion, democratic renewal requires actively engaging the next generation in governance. By involving young people in decision-making processes, we can harness their energy, ideas, and perspectives to create more inclusive, responsive, and effective democratic systems. Through education, participation mechanisms, technological innovation, and inclusive practices, we can ensure that the next generation is empowered to shape the future of their societies.

As we conclude this exploration of democratic renewal, the metaphorical seeds of democracy are being nurtured in the hands of the next generation. The chapters to come will delve into real-world examples, showcase successful youth-led initiatives, and continue our journey through the evolving landscape of democratic governance, guided by the principles of empowerment, inclusivity, and the unwavering belief that the future of democracy is entrusted to those who shape it today.

CHAPTER 20

DEMOCRATIC ADVERSITY:

NAVIGATING CHALLENGES WITH RESILIENCE

"The greatest glory in living lies not in never falling, but in rising every time we fall." – Nelson Mandela

Chapter 20 delves into the concept of democratic adversity, recognizing that the journey of governance is not without its trials. Resilient democracies navigate challenges with fortitude, learning from setbacks, and leveraging adversity as a catalyst for renewal, reform, and the continual evolution of the democratic ideal.

The Inevitability of Challenges

Envision a resilient democracy that acknowledges challenges not as indicators of failure but as inherent aspects of the democratic journey. Challenges may arise from external threats, internal conflicts, or the complexities of a rapidly changing world, but in their crucible lies the opportunity for democratic renewal.

Anticipating and Addressing Threats:

Resilient democracies proactively identify potential threats to their democratic fabric. Whether it be external influences, cyber threats, or internal divisions, they implement measures to safeguard against erosion of democratic principles.

Crisis Leadership: Navigating Storms

In times of crisis, democratic leaders become the captains steering the ship through turbulent waters. Picture a scenario where leaders rise to the occasion, displaying transparency, empathy, and decisiveness in the face of adversity, reinforcing the resilience of democratic governance.

Crisis Communication and Public Trust:

Communication becomes a linchpin during crises. Resilient democracies prioritize transparent communication, keeping the public informed, and addressing concerns promptly. In doing so, they foster trust and unity even in the most challenging circumstances.

Democratic Backsliding: Safeguarding Against Erosion

In the face of adversity, the specter of democratic backsliding may emerge. Visualize a democracy that actively safeguards against erosion of democratic norms, reinforcing the checks and balances that serve as bulwarks against autocratic tendencies.

Strengthening Institutions:

Resilient democracies prioritize the strengthening of

democratic institutions. This involves fortifying the independence of the judiciary, ensuring a free and robust media, and reinforcing the accountability mechanisms that form the backbone of democratic governance.

Inclusive Decision-Making: Uniting in Diversity

Adversity often tests the cohesion of diverse societies. In a resilient democracy, adversity becomes an opportunity to reinforce the principles of inclusion, ensuring that decision-making processes actively involve diverse voices and perspectives.

National Dialogues and Reconciliation Initiatives:

In the aftermath of crises, resilient democracies initiate national dialogues and reconciliation efforts. These endeavors provide spaces for healing, understanding, and forging a common path forward, fostering unity in diversity.

Learning from Setbacks: The Path to Renewal

Rather than viewing setbacks as permanent defeats, resilient democracies approach challenges as learning opportunities. Imagine a society that reflects on its mistakes, adapts to changing circumstances, and actively seeks renewal through a commitment to continuous improvement.

Post-Crisis Reforms:

The aftermath of adversity becomes a phase of introspection

and reform. Resilient democracies utilize the lessons learned from setbacks to implement reforms that enhance the responsiveness, inclusivity, and adaptability of their democratic systems.

Civic Resilience: The Role of an Informed Citizenry

In the face of adversity, the resilience of democracy is intricately tied to the resilience of its citizens. Envision a society where an informed and engaged citizenry actively participates in the democratic process, serving as a bulwark against the forces that seek to undermine democratic values.

Media Literacy and Critical Thinking:

Resilient democracies invest in media literacy and critical thinking education. An informed public, capable of discerning disinformation and critically evaluating information, becomes a potent force in upholding the integrity of democratic discourse.

Global Solidarity: United Against Threats

In an interconnected world, democratic adversity is not confined to national borders. Resilient democracies actively engage in global solidarity, recognizing that collaborative efforts are essential to address challenges that transcend individual nations.

International Cooperation in Crisis Response:

Resilient democracies contribute to international efforts in crisis response. Whether it be health crises, environmental challenges, or security threats, they actively participate in collaborative initiatives, recognizing that global challenges require global solutions.

Conclusion: Rising Stronger

As we conclude this exploration of democratic adversity, the essence becomes clear—resilience lies not in the absence of challenges but in the ability to navigate and overcome them. The chapters ahead will delve into case studies, showcase real-world examples, and continue our journey through the dynamic landscape of democratic governance, where each trial becomes a stepping stone toward a stronger, more resilient democracy.

CHAPTER 21

DEMOCRATIC LEGACY: SUSTAINING THE

FLAME OF LIBERTY

"The preservation of the sacred fire of liberty and the destiny of the republican model of government are justly considered as deeply, perhaps as finally, staked on the experiment entrusted to the hands of the American people."
– George Washington

Chapter 21 embarks on a contemplative journey, exploring the legacy of democracy—the enduring flame of liberty passed from one generation to the next. In the twilight of this exploration, we reflect on the responsibility to sustain, nurture, and continually enrich the democratic legacy for the benefit of present and future societies.

Upholding Democratic Values

Envision a society where the core tenets of democracy are not just words but guiding principles embedded in the collective conscience. Resilient democracies recognize that upholding values such as freedom, equality, justice, and the rule of law is not a one-time commitment but an ongoing endeavor.

Education in Democratic Values:

The transmission of democratic values begins in the classroom. Schools and educational institutions play a pivotal role in instilling a sense of civic responsibility, respect for diversity, and a deep understanding of democratic principles in the hearts and minds of the younger generation.

Civic Engagement as a Way of Life

In a thriving democracy, civic engagement is not a sporadic activity but a way of life. Picture a society where citizens actively participate in community initiatives, civil discourse, and decision-making processes, recognizing that democracy flourishes when individuals take ownership of their collective destiny.

Community-Based Democracy:

Resilient democracies foster a sense of community ownership. Local governance becomes an arena where citizens actively engage in shaping the policies and practices that directly impact their daily lives, creating a democratic ecosystem that is responsive and inclusive.

Intergenerational Dialogue: Bridging Past and Future

As societies evolve, the legacy of democracy is passed from one generation to the next. Visualize a scenario where dialogue between generations is not just a formality but a dynamic exchange of ideas, experiences, and wisdom, ensuring that the flame of liberty is sustained and adapted for contemporary challenges.

Mentorship Programs and Civic Education Initiatives: Formalized mentorship programs and civic education initiatives become channels for intergenerational dialogue.

These initiatives bridge the gap between the seasoned wisdom of those who have witnessed the evolution of democracy and the fresh perspectives of the next generation.

Environmental Democracy: Guardianship of the Planet

In the legacy of democracy, envision a commitment to environmental stewardship. Resilient democracies recognize the interconnectedness of environmental health and democratic well-being. Policies and practices are aligned to ensure that the preservation of the planet becomes an integral aspect of the democratic legacy.

Sustainable Development Goals (SDGs) as Democratic Imperatives:

Resilient democracies actively contribute to global initiatives like the Sustainable Development Goals (SDGs). They recognize that environmental sustainability, social equity, and economic prosperity are not mutually exclusive but essential components of a democratic legacy.

Social Justice: The Moral Compass of Democracy

A sustainable democratic legacy is rooted in principles of social justice. Imagine a society where inclusivity, equality, and the eradication of systemic injustices are not just aspirations but the driving force behind policies, institutions, and the collective conscience of the nation.

Restorative Justice and Equal Opportunity Programs:

Resilient democracies actively pursue restorative justice initiatives and equal opportunity programs. They address historical injustices, dismantle systemic biases, and create a society where every individual, regardless of background, has an equal chance to thrive.

Technological Ethics: Balancing Progress and Principles

In the digital age, the democratic legacy extends to the ethical use of technology. Picture a society where technological advancements are not pursued at the expense of democratic values but aligned with principles of privacy, transparency, and the protection of individual freedoms.

Digital Bill of Rights and Ethical Tech Governance:

Resilient democracies establish digital bills of rights and ethical tech governance frameworks. These mechanisms ensure that the benefits of technological progress are harnessed while safeguarding against abuses that could compromise democratic principles.

International Collaboration: Guardians of Global Democracy

The legacy of democracy is not confined by borders. Envision a scenario where resilient democracies actively collaborate on the global stage, sharing experiences, expertise, and resources to fortify democratic values in the face of shared challenges.

Democratic Alliances and Global Governance:

Resilient democracies contribute to international forums,

alliances, and governance structures. They play an active role in shaping a global landscape where human rights, peace, and democratic principles are upheld as universal values.

Continuous Reform: The Dynamic Nature of Democracy

The legacy of democracy is not static; it is a dynamic force that requires continuous reform and adaptation. Visualize a society where the capacity for self-reflection, reform, and renewal is ingrained in the democratic ethos, ensuring that the flame of liberty remains bright and unwavering.

Adaptive Governance Mechanisms:

Resilient democracies institutionalize adaptive governance mechanisms. They actively seek feedback, anticipate challenges, and implement reforms that align with the evolving needs and expectations of their citizens.

Conclusion: The Enduring Flame

As we conclude this exploration of the democratic legacy, the enduring flame of liberty remains aglow. In the chapters ahead, we will delve into case studies, examine real-world examples, and continue our journey through the ever-evolving landscape of democratic governance. The legacy of democracy is not a relic of the past but a living, breathing force that guides societies toward a future where the principles of freedom, equality, and justice continue to illuminate the path forward.

CHAPTER 22

DEMOCRATIC HORIZON: NAVIGATING THE

UNCHARTED FUTURE

"The future is not there waiting for us. We create it by the power of imagination." – Vijay Govindarajan

Chapter 22 propels our exploration into the democratic horizon, a realm where the uncharted future awaits. In this chapter, we venture into the unknown, contemplating the possibilities, challenges, and potential transformations that lie ahead for democratic governance. The horizon beckons, and resilient democracies stand ready to shape the contours of the democratic future.

The Dynamics of Technological Progress

Envision a future where technological advancements continue to redefine the democratic landscape. Resilient democracies adapt to emerging technologies, harnessing their potential while mitigating risks to uphold the principles of privacy, transparency, and individual freedoms.

AI and Ethical Governance:

Resilient democracies establish frameworks for the ethical use of artificial intelligence (AI). They navigate the challenges posed by automated decision-making, ensuring accountability, and protecting against biases that may impact democratic values.

The Evolution of Civic Engagement

In the democratic future, civic engagement undergoes a metamorphosis. Picture a society where digital platforms, augmented reality, and other innovations create new avenues for citizens to actively participate in governance, transcending traditional boundaries and enhancing inclusivity.

Virtual Democracy and E-Governance:

Resilient democracies embrace virtual democracy and e-governance, leveraging digital tools to facilitate real-time citizen participation. Virtual town halls, digital voting mechanisms, and online forums become integral components of a dynamic democratic ecosystem.

Climate Change and Democratic Resilience

The future is marked by the increasing urgency of addressing climate change. Imagine resilient democracies at the forefront of sustainable policies, global collaboration, and innovative solutions, recognizing the intrinsic connection between environmental health and the well-being of democratic societies.

Green Governance Initiatives:

Resilient democracies pioneer green governance initiatives, prioritizing policies that address climate challenges. They collaborate on a global scale to ensure the sustainability of democratic ideals in the face of environmental crises.

Inclusive Global Governance

The democratic future envisions an era of enhanced international collaboration. Picture resilient democracies actively participating in global governance structures, fostering diplomatic initiatives, and contributing to the development of a more inclusive and equitable world order.

Democratic Diplomacy 2.0:

In the future, democratic diplomacy evolves to address complex global challenges. Resilient democracies engage in diplomatic efforts that go beyond national interests, promoting democratic values, human rights, and collective well-being on the global stage.

Strengthening Democratic Institutions

As societies evolve, the institutions safeguarding democracy must evolve as well. Envision a future where resilient democracies continually strengthen the independence of judiciaries, reinforce checks and balances, and adapt governance structures to the changing needs of their citizens.

Digital Democracy Safeguards:

Resilient democracies implement robust safeguards in the digital realm. Cybersecurity measures, protection against disinformation, and the ethical use of technology become integral components in preserving the integrity of democratic institutions.

Social Equity in the Digital Age

In the democratic future, the pursuit of social equity becomes even more pronounced. Visualize societies where technological advancements are harnessed to bridge the digital divide, ensuring that the benefits of progress are accessible to all, regardless of socioeconomic status.

Tech for Social Good Initiatives:

Resilient democracies champion initiatives that leverage technology for social good. From digital literacy programs to initiatives promoting inclusive innovation, they actively work to mitigate the potential negative impacts of technological progress on marginalized communities.

Democratic Education for the Future

The future demands an education system that equips citizens with the skills, knowledge, and ethical considerations necessary for active participation in democracy. Picture resilient democracies investing in transformative educational approaches that nurture critical thinking, adaptability, and civic responsibility.

Civic Education 2.0:

Resilient democracies reimagine civic education, incorporating digital literacy, global awareness, and participatory learning. Educational institutions become dynamic hubs for preparing citizens to navigate the complexities of the democratic future.

Conclusion: Shaping the Uncharted Future

As we conclude this journey into the democratic horizon, the essence becomes clear—resilient democracies are not passive spectators of the future; they are active architects, shaping the uncharted landscapes that lie ahead. The chapters to come will delve into unfolding narratives, examine real-time innovations, and continue our exploration through the ever-evolving tapestry of democratic governance—a journey where the democratic flame is not merely sustained but illuminated anew with each passing era.

In the grand tapestry of human history, the story of democracy is both a testament to the enduring spirit of freedom and a call to action for each generation. As we navigate the currents of the present and gaze into the uncharted future, let the principles of democracy guide our collective journey.

Democracy is not a static entity confined to the pages of history; it is a living, breathing force shaped by the actions, aspirations, and resilience of its participants. The chapters we've explored—from the origins and challenges to the triumphs and innovations—illustrate the dynamic nature of democratic governance.

In the face of adversity, democracy has proven itself resilient, a system capable of learning, adapting, and renewing its commitment to the fundamental values of liberty, equality, and justice. The legacy of democracy is entrusted to each generation, a flame passed from one hand to the next, to be sustained and elevated.

As we step into the democratic horizon, let us embrace the

responsibilities that come with the privileges of self-governance. Let our actions reflect the understanding that democracy is not a guarantee but a continuous effort, requiring the engagement, vigilance, and imagination of its citizens.

May the democratic flame burn brightly in the hearts and minds of individuals around the world. Through informed participation, empathetic discourse, and a commitment to justice, may we shape a future where democracy not only endures but thrives—a beacon of hope, a guardian of freedom, and a testament to the collective power of people shaping their destiny.

In the final analysis, the true measure of democracy's success lies not only in its longevity but in its capacity to create societies where every voice is heard, every individual is respected, and the pursuit of a better tomorrow is a shared endeavor. The democratic journey is perpetual, and as we turn the page to the next chapter, let us continue to write a story that celebrates the human spirit and the enduring ideals of democracy.

In "Black Democracy: The Tragedy of Non-Compliance with Electoral Legislations," the tumultuous journey of democratic governance takes center stage. Unveiling the complex tapestry of challenges faced by nations striving for political freedom, this book delves into the intricacies of electoral processes and the profound consequences of non-compliance.

From the roots of democracy to contemporary struggles, each chapter unfurls a different layer of the narrative. Historical anecdotes, famous quotes, and global perspectives weave together to illustrate the impact of neglecting electoral legislations on the very essence of democracy. The tragic divergence from democratic principles becomes a focal point, prompting readers to reflect on the consequences of faltering in the fundamental duty of compliance.

As the chapters unfold, "Black Democracy" navigates the global landscape while grounding its exploration in the local nuances that shape the democratic experiences of nations. The book serves as a poignant exploration of the challenges faced by Black democracies, shedding light on the vulnerabilities that can erode the foundations of political freedom.

Through a lens that is both critical and hopeful, this book invites readers to confront the tragedies of non-compliance, prompting a deeper understanding of the responsibilities that come with the privilege of self-governance. "Black Democracy" is not just a title—it's a call to action, urging individuals to engage, reflect, and actively participate in safeguarding the democratic ideals that form the bedrock of a just and equitable society.

Call to Action: Safeguarding Democratic Principles Through Adherence to Electoral Legislations

1. Educate and Raise Awareness: Promote public understanding of electoral legislations, their importance in upholding democratic principles, and the potential consequences of non-compliance. Conduct civic education campaigns, workshops, and public forums to inform citizens about their rights and responsibilities in the electoral process.

2. Strengthen Electoral Laws: Advocate for the development and enhancement of robust electoral laws that ensure transparency, fairness, and inclusivity. Encourage lawmakers to review and update existing legislations to address emerging challenges, such as the influence of technology on elections.

3. Independent Oversight and Enforcement: Advocate for the establishment of independent oversight bodies or commissions responsible for monitoring and enforcing compliance with electoral legislations. These bodies should have the authority to investigate complaints, impose penalties for non-compliance, and ensure the integrity of the electoral process.

4. Political Party Accountability: Encourage political parties to adhere to electoral legislations and promote internal mechanisms for accountability. Political parties should develop and enforce codes of conduct that guide the behavior

of their members, candidates, and officials during election campaigns.

5. Transparent Campaign Financing: Advocate for transparent and accountable campaign financing systems. Support measures that require political parties and candidates to disclose their sources of funding and expenditures to prevent undue influence and promote fairness in electoral competition.

6. Strengthen Election Administration: Support efforts to enhance the capacity, independence, and professionalism of election management bodies. Ensure that election officials are adequately trained in electoral legislations and best practices, and have the necessary resources to conduct elections efficiently and impartially.

7. Voter Education and Engagement: Promote voter education initiatives to ensure citizens understand their rights, voting procedures, and the importance of their participation in the electoral process. Encourage voter registration drives and initiatives that facilitate access to information for all eligible voters.

8. Monitor and Report Irregularities: Encourage civil society organizations, media, and citizens to actively monitor the

electoral process and report any irregularities or violations of electoral legislations. Support the establishment of mechanisms for reporting complaints and ensure that they are investigated promptly and impartially.

9. International Cooperation: Foster international cooperation and exchange of best practices in electoral legislations and enforcement. Engage with international organizations, such as the United Nations and regional bodies, to promote standards and guidelines for electoral integrity.

10. Public Engagement and Advocacy: Mobilize public support for the adherence to electoral legislations through advocacy campaigns, public demonstrations, and grassroots movements. Engage with civil society organizations, media outlets, and community leaders to amplify the message of safeguarding democratic principles.

By actively promoting and adhering to electoral legislations, we can protect the integrity of electoral processes, uphold democratic principles, and ensure that the voice and will of the people are respected. Together, let us work towards building inclusive, transparent, and accountable electoral systems that foster trust, promote civic participation, and safeguard our democratic ideals.

In the face of evolving challenges to democratic governance, our collective responsibility becomes paramount. The bedrock of a thriving democracy lies in the steadfast adherence to electoral legislations—the rules that govern the very essence of our political system. As we navigate the intricate landscape of civic duty, let this be a resounding call to action:

1. Educate and Empower:

- Foster awareness about the importance of electoral legislations in safeguarding democratic principles.

- Empower citizens through civic education programs, ensuring they understand their rights and responsibilities.

2. Promote Inclusivity:

- Advocate for inclusive electoral laws that foster representation from diverse backgrounds.

- Strive for equitable access to the electoral process, removing barriers that may hinder participation.

3. Advocate for Transparency:

- Demand transparency in electoral processes, from campaign financing to ballot counting.

- Support initiatives that ensure public access to accurate

and timely information throughout the electoral cycle.

4. Combat Disinformation:

- Actively counter disinformation campaigns that undermine the integrity of the electoral process.

- Promote media literacy to empower citizens in discerning credible information from misinformation.

5. Hold Leaders Accountable:

- Demand accountability from elected officials, urging them to adhere to and respect electoral legislations.

- Support mechanisms that ensure consequences for those who breach democratic norms.

6. Participate Actively:

- Exercise your right to vote and encourage others to do the same.

- Engage in civil discourse, fostering an environment where diverse perspectives contribute to informed decision-making.

7. Support Electoral Reforms:

- Advocate for reforms that enhance the fairness,

transparency, and efficiency of electoral processes.

- Engage in dialogue with policymakers to address gaps in existing legislations and adapt to emerging challenges.

8. Embrace Civic Responsibility:

- Recognize that the strength of democracy rests on the shoulders of an informed and engaged citizenry.

- Embrace civic responsibility beyond elections, actively participating in community initiatives and decision-making processes.

9. Build Coalitions for Change:

- Form alliances with like-minded individuals and organizations to amplify the call for adherence to electoral legislations.

- Mobilize communities to collectively advocate for the preservation of democratic principles.

10. Safeguard Against Voter Suppression:

- Combat efforts to suppress voter participation, advocating for measures that protect the rights of all eligible voters.

- Support initiatives that ensure fair and accessible electoral systems for every citizen.

11. Engage the Youth:

- Empower the next generation with the knowledge and tools to actively participate in shaping the democratic future.

- Create platforms for youth involvement in electoral processes and policy discussions.

12. Celebrate Democratic Values:

- Uphold the values of democracy—freedom, equality, justice—as guiding principles in everyday actions.

- Celebrate and promote democratic achievements, fostering a sense of pride in our shared commitment to governance by the people.

As we embark on this collective journey, let us remember that the preservation of democracy is a continuous effort, requiring the active involvement of every citizen. By championing adherence to electoral legislations, we fortify the foundations of democracy, ensuring that the flame of liberty burns bright for generations to come. Together, let us be the guardians of democratic principles and architects of a future where the voice of the people resounds in every electoral decision.

GLOSSARY

1. Democracy: A system of government where power is vested in the hands of the people, either directly or through elected representatives.

2. Non-Compliance: Failure or refusal to adhere to laws, regulations, or established norms, particularly in the context of electoral legislations.

3. Electoral Legislations: Laws and regulations governing the conduct of elections, encompassing issues like voter eligibility, campaigning rules, and the electoral process.

4. Tragedy: A deeply distressing or disastrous event, in this context referring to the negative consequences of not complying with electoral legislations on the democratic process.

5. Tapestry: Metaphorically used to represent the intricate and interconnected elements of the democratic system, suggesting a complex and interwoven fabric.

6. Divergence: The act of moving or extending in different directions; in this context, the deviation from democratic principles.

7. Nuances: Subtle variations or shades of meaning, often referring to the subtle complexities within the context of electoral legislations.

8. Global Perspective: Considering issues from a worldwide viewpoint, acknowledging the interconnectedness of democracies around the world.

9. Local Context: Understanding and interpreting issues within the specific circumstances or conditions of a particular community or region.

10. Consequences: The results or effects of a particular action, in this case, the outcomes of non-compliance with electoral legislations.

11. Political Freedom: The state of being free from oppressive restrictions imposed by the government or political authority.

12. Vulnerabilities: Weaknesses or susceptibilities that can be exploited, indicating potential threats to the stability of democratic systems.

13. Foundations: The underlying principles or base on which something stands, referring to the fundamental principles of democracy.

14. Equitable Society: A society that is fair, just, and provides equal opportunities and treatment for all its members.

15. Responsibilities: Duties and obligations, especially those associated with active citizenship in a democratic system.

16. Metaphor: A figure of speech in which a word or phrase is applied to something to which it is not literally applicable, used here to describe the concept of a tapestry representing democracy.

17. Critical Reflection: Thoughtful and careful consideration of issues, encouraging a deep and analytical understanding.

18. Privilege: A special advantage or immunity, in this context referring to the privilege of self-governance in a democracy.

19. Political Landscape: The overall political environment, including the parties, ideologies, and power dynamics within a given region or country.

20. Inclusion: The act of including or being included within a group or structure, often used in the context of ensuring diverse representation in democratic processes.

21. Accountability: The obligation to accept responsibility for one's actions, particularly in the context of elected officials being answerable to the public.

22. Transparency: The quality of being open and honest, often used to describe the accessibility of information in political processes.

23. Citizenship: The status of being a member of a particular

country, often entailing rights and responsibilities.

24. Political Activism: The participation in or support for activities aimed at achieving political change, often through protest or advocacy.

25. Civil Discourse: Respectful and reasoned discussion of issues, emphasizing open communication and understanding in the democratic process.

26. Disinformation: False or misleading information spread with the intent to deceive, often impacting the integrity of electoral processes.

27. Civic Duty: The responsibility of citizens to actively participate in the democratic process, such as voting and staying informed.

28. Societal Resilience: The capacity of a society to adapt and recover from challenges, including those posed by non-compliance with electoral legislations.

29. Public Trust: The confidence and reliance that citizens place in their government and democratic institutions.

30. Reform: The process of making changes to improve a system, often applied to political or electoral systems to address shortcomings.

REFERENCE

Adebayo, P F & J Shola Omotola. 2007. 'Public Perception of Nigeria's 2007 General Elections'. Journal of African Elections 6(2), October.

Adejomobi, S. 2007. 'When Votes Do Not Count: The 2007 General Elections in Nigeria'. News from Nordic African Institute, No 2, May.

———— & M Kehinde. 2007. 'Building Democracy without Democrats?: Political Parties and Threats of Democratic Reversal in Nigeria'. Journal of African Elections 6(2), October.

Agbaje, A & S Adejumobi. 2006. 'Do Votes Count? The Travail of Electoral Politics in Nigeria'. Africa Development XXXI (3).

Agbo, A. 2010. 'Red card for Mr President. Civil society groups insist that President Umaru Yar'Adua leaves the scene for Acting President Goodluck Jonathan to take full charge'. Tell, 22 March.

Agyeman-Duah, B. 2005. Elections and Electoral Politics in Ghana's Fourth Republic. Critical Perspective 18, CDD-Ghana, July.

Akintunde, K. 2008. 'Furore over Electoral Reform White Paper'. Newswatch, 24 September. Available at: www.newswatchngr.com/index.php?option=com_ content&task=view&id=755&Itemid=47

Anonymous. 2010. 'Obasanjo's Retort and the Death of Imagination'. Available at: www.nigeriavillagesquare.com/articles/adebowale-oriku/obasanjosretort-and-the-death-of-imagination.html

Berinsky, A J. 2005. 'The Perverse Consequences of Electoral Reform in the United States'. American Politics Research 33(4), July. Birch, S. 2008. 'Electoral institutions and popular confidence in electoral processes: A cross-national analysis'. Electoral Studies 27(1).

Browne, O. 2004. 'The Electoral Machine: The Bureaucracy and the Electoral Process in the Making of Nigeria's Fourth Republic'. In L Olurode & R Anifowose (eds). Issues in Nigeria's 1999 General Elections. Lagos: John West and Rebonik Publications.

National Democratic Institute. 2007. 'This is Not the Will of Nigerians'. Text of a report of the NDI, a Washington-based organisation led by Madeleine Albright, former US Secretary of State, on the 2007 Nigerian Election.

Nwosu, H. 2008. Laying the Foundation for Nigeria's Democracy: My Account of June 12, 1993 Presidential Election and its Annulment. Lagos: Macmillan.

Oguntola, S. 2010. 'Obasanjo Blasphemed Jesus, Say Okonkwo, Osu, Others'. The Nation, 2 May. Available at: thenationonlineng.net/web2/articles/45061/1/ Obasanjo-blasphemed-Jesus-says-Okonkwo-Osu-others-/Page1.html

Omotola, J S. 2009a. '"Garrison" Democracy in Nigeria: The 2007 General Elections and the Prospects of Democratic Consolidation'. Commonwealth and Comparative Politics 47(2).

1. Britannica. (n.d.). Optimates and Populares | Roman Senate, Patricians, Plebeians. Retrieved from https://www.britannica.com/topic/Optimates-and-Populares

2. Bing. (n.d.). The Populares and Optimates in Ancient Rome. Retrieved from https://bing.com/search?q=The+Populares+and+Optimates+in+Ancient+Rome

3. History Forum. (n.d.). The Optimates and the Populares. Retrieved from https://historum.com/t/the-optimates-and-the-populares.94005/

4. Wikiwand. (n.d.). Optimates and Populares. Retrieved from https://www.wikiwand.com/en/Optimates

5. ThoughtCo. (n.d.). Ancient Roman History: The Optimates. Retrieved from https://www.thoughtco.com/ancient-roman-history-optimates-119359

6. Library for Kids. (n.d.). Optimates and Populares: The Elite Struggle for the Control of Rome. Retrieved from https://libraryforkids.com/optimates-and-populares-the-elite-struggle-for-the-control-of-rome/

7. Wikipedia. (n.d.). Optimates and Populares. Retrieved from https://en.wikipedia.org/wiki/Optimates_and_populares

8. Freedom House. (n.d.). Policy Recommendations: Strengthening Democracy. Retrieved from https://freedomhouse.org/policy-recommendations/strengthening-democracy-abroad

9. The Hill. (n.d.). Democrats' Increasing Disregard for Democracy. Retrieved from https://thehill.com/opinion/white-house/3620228-democrats-increasing-disregard-for-democracy/

10. Transnational Institute. (n.d.). Disregard for Human Rights, Dignity, Democratic Values, and Justice... Retrieved from https://www.tni.org/en/article/disregard-for-human-rights-dignity-democratic-values-and-justice-will-hurt-us-to-the-core

11. Big Think. (n.d.). How the Medici Family Created and Lost Their Banking Empire. Retrieved from https://bigthink.com/culture-religion/how-the-medici-family-created-and-lost-their-banking-empire/

12. History. (n.d.). Medici Family: Cosimo, Lorenzo & Catherine. Retrieved from https://www.history.com/topics/renaissance/medici-family

13. Britannica. (n.d.). Pazzi Conspiracy | Renaissance, Florence, Lorenzo de' Medici. Retrieved from https://www.britannica.com/event/Pazzi-conspiracy

14. The Vintage News. (n.d.). Renaissance Italy's Most Powerful Family. Retrieved from https://www.thevintagenews.com/2018/11/17/the-medici/

15. The Tuscan Mom. (n.d.). The Medici In Florence –

Where To See Their Influence + Map. Retrieved from https://thetuscanmom.com/medici-in-florence/

16. Bing. (n.d.). How Did the Medici Family Lose Power in Florence? Retrieved from https://bing.com/search?q=How+did+the+Medici+family+lose+power+in+Florence%3f

17. Encyclopedia.com. (n.d.). Medici Family. Retrieved from https://www.encyclopedia.com/history/encyclopedias-almanacs-transcripts-and-maps/medici-family

18. Britannica. (n.d.). Optimates and Populares | Roman Senate, Patricians, Plebeians. Retrieved from https://www.britannica.com/topic/Optimates-and-Populares

19. Wikipedia. (n.d.). Optimates and Populares. Retrieved from https://en.wikipedia.org/wiki/Optimates_and_populares

20. History Forum. (n.d.). The Optimates and the Populares. Retrieved from https://historum.com/t/the-optimates-and-the-populares.94005/

21. Bing. (n.d.). The Populares and Optimates in Ancient

Rome. Retrieved from https://bing.com/search?q=The+Populares+and+Optimates+in+Ancient+Rome

22. ThoughtCo. (n.d.). Ancient Roman History: The Optimates. Retrieved from https://www.thoughtco.com/ancient-roman-history-optimates-119359

23. Library for Kids. (n.d.). Optimates and Populares: The Elite Struggle for the Control of Rome. Retrieved from https://libraryforkids.com/optimates-and-populares-the-elite-struggle-for-the-control-of-rome/

24. The Collector. (n.d.). The Medici Family: Ultimate Power and Legacy In The Renaissance. Retrieved from https://www.thecollector.com/the-medici-family-legacy/

25. Daily History. (n.d.). How Did the de Medici Contribute to the Renaissance. Retrieved from https://www.dailyhistory.org/How_did_the_de_Medici_contribute_to_the_Renaissance

26. History. (n.d.). Medici Family: Cosimo, Lorenzo & Catherine. Retrieved from

https://www.history.com/topics/renaissance/medici-family

27. ISI

 Florence. (n.d.). The Medici Legacy: Florence's Iconic Family. Retrieved from https://isiflorence.org/the-medici-legacy-florences-iconic-family/

28. Bing. (n.d.). The Medici Influence in Renaissance Florence. Retrieved from https://bing.com/search?q=The+Medici+Influence+in+Renaissance+Florence

29. The Tuscan Mom. (n.d.). The Medici In Florence – Where To See Their Influence + Map. Retrieved from https://thetuscanmom.com/medici-in-florence/

30. Classroom Rick Steves. (n.d.). Medici Family and Florentine Renaissance. Retrieved from https://classroom.ricksteves.com/videos/medici-family-and-florentine-renaissance

31. Academia.edu. (n.d.). The African Origins of Democracy. Retrieved from

https://www.academia.edu/45679749/The_African_Origins_
of_Democracy

32. National Academies. (n.d.). The Movement Toward Democracy in Africa. Retrieved from https://nap.nationalacademies.org/read/2041/chapter/3

33. Wikipedia. (n.d.). Democracy in Africa. Retrieved from https://en.wikipedia.org/wiki/Democracy_in_Africa

34. DOI. (n.d.). Retrieved from https://doi.org/10.20935/AL414

35. LawPavilion. (n.d.). What a Petitioner Must Show to Prove Substantial Non-Compliance. Retrieved from https://lawpavilion.com/blog/what-a-petitioner-must-show-to-prove-substantial-non-compliance-with-the-provisions-of-the-electoral-act-and-approved-guidelines/

36. Constitution Center. (n.d.). Explaining How Congress Settles Electoral College Disputes. Retrieved from https://constitutioncenter.org/blog/explaining-how-congress-settles-electoral-college-disputes

37. The Regulatory Review. (n.d.). A Case for Mandatory Voting. Retrieved from https://www.theregreview.org/2021/07/07/sheppard-case-for-mandatory-voting/

38. The ICIR Nigeria. (n.d.). 2023: INEC Warns Political Parties Against Non-Compliance. Retrieved from https://www.icirnigeria.org/2023-inec-warns-political-parties-against-flouting-electoral-act/

39. European Commission. (n.d.). Democracy and Electoral Rights. Retrieved from https://commission.europa.eu/strategy-and-policy/policies/justice-and-fundamental-rights/eu-citizenship/democracy-and-electoral-rights_en

40. LawPavilion. (n.d.). Requirement of the Law Where There Is an Allegation of Corrupt Practices and Substantial Non-Compliance. Retrieved from https://lawpavilion.com/blog/requirement-of-the-law-where-there-is-an-allegation-of-corrupt-practices-and-substantial-non-compliance-with-the-provisions-of-the-electoral-act-2010-in-an-election/

41. International Institute for Democracy and Electoral Assistance (IDEA). (n.d.). Inside the Courts and Challenging

Election Outcomes. Retrieved from https://www.idea.int/news/inside-courts-and-challenging-election-outcomes

42. IDEA. (n.d.). International Obligations for Elections. Retrieved from https://www.idea.int/sites/default/files/publications/international-obligations-for-elections.pdf

43. IDEA. (n.d.). Best Practices for Ensuring Compliance with Registration and Voting. Retrieved from https://elections.ca/content.aspx?section=res&dir=cons/comp/bp&document=p5&lang=e

44. IDEA. (n.d.). International Electoral Standards. Retrieved from https://www.idea.int/sites/default/files/publications/international-electoral-standards-guidelines-for-reviewing-the-legal-framework-of-elections.pdf

45. IDEA. (n.d.). Best Practices for Ensuring Compliance with Registration and Voting. Retrieved from https://elections.ca/content.aspx?section=res&dir=cons/comp/bp&document=p4&lang=e

46. IDEA. (n.d.). Retrieved from http://www.idea.int/publications/pub_electoral_main.html

47. World History Encyclopedia. (n.d.). Athenian Democracy. Retrieved from https://www.worldhistory.org/Athenian_Democracy/

48. Wikipedia. (n.d.). Athenian Democracy. Retrieved from https://en.wikipedia.org/wiki/Athenian_democracy

49. History. (n.d.). Ancient Greek Democracy. Retrieved from https://www.history.com/topics/ancient-greece/ancient-greece-democracy

50. Wikipedia. (n.d.). Retrieved from https://en.wikipedia.org/wiki/Athenian_democracy

51. Wikipedia. (n.d.). Election Law. Retrieved from https://en.wikipedia.org/wiki/Election_law

52. National Archives. (n.d.). Electoral College History. Retrieved from https://www.archives.gov/electoral-college/history

53. History. (n.d.). Voting Rights Milestones in America: A Timeline. Retrieved from https://www.history.com/news/voting-rights-timeline

54. Constitution Center. (n.d.). The Evolution of Voting Rights in America. Retrieved from https://constitutioncenter.org/blog/the-evolution-of-voting-rights-in-america

55. IFES - The International Foundation for Electoral Systems. (n.d.). Electoral Legal & Regulatory Frameworks. Retrieved from https://www.ifes.org/our-expertise/election-integrity/electoral-legal-regulatory-frameworks

56. IDEA. (n.d.). International Obligations for Elections: Guidelines for Legal Frameworks. Retrieved from https://www.idea.int/publications/catalogue/international-obligations-elections-guidelines-legal-frameworks

57. ACE Project. (n.d.). Legal Framework of Electoral Integrity. Retrieved from https://aceproject.org/ace-en/topics/ei/eib

58. IDEA. (n.d.). International Electoral Standards. Retrieved from

https://www.idea.int/sites/default/files/publications/internatio
nal-electoral-standards-guidelines-for-reviewing-the-legal-
framework-of-elections.pdf

59. LawPavilion. (n.d.). What a Petitioner Must Show to
Prove Substantial Non-Compliance. Retrieved from
https://lawpavilion.com/blog/what-a-petitioner-must-show-
to-prove-substantial-non-compliance-with-the-provisions-of-
the-electoral-act-and-approved-guidelines/

60. CJ Okoye Law View. (n.d.). Allegation of Non-
Compliance with the Electoral Act. Retrieved from
https://cjokoyelawview.com/component/k2/item/9226-
allegation-of-non-compliance-with-the-electoral-act-
whether-a-petitioner-who-alleges-non-compliance-with-the-
provisions-of-the-electoral-act-must-show-how-it-
substantially-affected-the-result-of-the-election

61. LawPavilion. (n.d.). Requirement of the Law Where
There Is an Allegation of Corrupt Practices and Substantial
Non-Compliance. Retrieved from
https://lawpavilion.com/blog/requirement-of-the-law-where-
there-is-an-allegation-of-corrupt-practices-and-substantial-
non-compliance-with-the-provisions-of

BLACK DEMOCRACY

About the Authors

Okey Ezeala is a University of Abuja trained Economist, public policy Analyst, Youth Activist and currently the Publicity Secretary of the All Progressives Congress - Abia State, Nigeria.

A renowned Philanthropist and Managing Director of El-Halal Infrastructures Ltd, Abuja. He is a model family man, community Chief and prolific writer with special interest in leadership, human rights, rule of law and order.

His best sellers include; Tyranny of the Weak, The Teenage Wish, ODIUKO the mother Africa needs etc.

Oko Obasi, a Nigerian politician, human activist, natural born leader, mentor, social engineer, and inspirational motivator. He is also a devoted Christian and a family man. He is happily married to Ifeyinwa Peace Igbokwe Obasi and they have five sons. His first literary work is called "Marriage Reloaded"

Other books by him include: Effective Communication in Hospital Environment, Pinocchio Syndrome, Take Action, Goshen Exclusion and the novel Just one day.